CRACKING the MAN CODE

How You Can Take Bold Steps Toward Becoming a New Man of God Today

---

by PETE MCKENZIE & PHIL VAN HORN

Editorial assistance by Mike Yorkey (www.mikeyorkey.com) and Heidi Moss

Cover and interior design by Emily Muse Morelli

For information on Pete McKenzie and Phil Van Horn or to book a speaking engagement, please contact Phil Van Horn at ballphild@gmail.com or by texting 818-517-5880.

TABLE OF CONTENTS

A NOTE TO THE READER

from Phil Van Horn

F ive years ago, Pete McKenzie and I sat down together and started writing *Cracking the Man Code*.

Immediately a storm of death and loss raged through our lives. We were aware that the Book of Job in the Old Testament was the biblical baseline of death, loss, and suffering, and everything that happened to Job seemed to happen to us.

It all started when Pete's beloved wife, Suzan, came down with breast cancer. An aggressive fight—chemotherapy, radiation—appeared to cure her, but after a couple of years, the breast cancer returned with a vengeance. Suzan, the youngest seventy-year-old you'd ever want to know, fought valiantly until the day she died on August 2, 2017, but Pete and I knew that Jesus welcomed her into His arms.

Pete and Suzan were blessed to share fifty years together. The courage and faith that Pete displayed during Suzan's heroic battles was a sterling testimony to his faith in a living Savior.

As for me, I barely have the courage to admit that my business crashed and we lost our home in the last five years. My wife, Lecia, and I were even more stunned to lose an overwhelming number of family members and friends to suicide (although one miraculously survived), cancer (prostate, lung, and pancreatic), and the worst military friendly-fire incident in Afghanistan.

At one point, Lecia counted ten deaths in a year and a half. I stopped counting after more than thirty deaths over a four-year period, which also included a heroin overdose. The incredible number of crisis phone calls, prayerful deathbed visits, and funeral services numbed us.

Just as distressing was witnessing the impact of Parkinson's disease and short-term memory loss from Alzheimer's disease on my mother. We also learned of tremendous financial and health problems that my mother-in-law concealed from us, and we had to step in and help her get back on her feet—though at times we acted against her own wishes.

And then Lecia and I received the fright of our lives when we learned that our daughter, Kari, and son, Brandon, came within inches of losing both of their lives *in the same night, in two separate states*, in what police believed was a gang-initiation armed robbery in Los Angeles and a murder-by-suicide bridge-jumper in Michigan.

Months before, our daughter survived a wrong-way driver incident that forced the car she was driving to crash into a building. Months later, our son survived a high-speed crash in which, police say, the other car was traveling near 80 miles-per-hour and barrel-rolled after contact.

Taken all together, the events of the last five years obliterated our faith-filled, middle-class lifestyle. We lived Job's "great sorrow." It occurred to me that Satan was throwing the kitchen sink at Lecia and myself as well as Suzan and Pete.

We had plenty of reasons to pray. We had plenty of reasons to trust in God because nearly everything that we cherished was stripped away. We had plenty of reasons to stay on our knees.

The book that you're holding in your hands, *Cracking the Man Code*, comes out of the ashes of these disappointments and setbacks, but we remain resolute that God is in control and He has a plan for good with our lives.

We dedicate this book to Pete's wife, Suzan McKenzie, because of her lifetime of support for Pete's ministry to men, which now includes you as a reader of *Cracking the Man Code*.

INTRODUCTION

Men are born with a code. We call it the "Man Code." Family and school teach the Man Code early in life. Later, culture reinforces and even alters the Code. Culture is greatly influenced by secular, liberal, and feminine ideology.

Unfortunately, this culturally influenced Man Code does not serve the average guy very well. The Man Code does not support the spiritual nature that God has created in him. Man, to the contrary, was born with a sinful nature. That contradiction, as well as a longing for reconciliation, leaves him unprotected and on an island in a very dangerous and difficult world.

"MEN HAVE BEEN MARGINALIZED IN OUR CULTURE TODAY."

—WILLIAM BENNETT, former Secretary of Education
under President Reagan, pundit and author

This book, *Cracking the Man Code,* is about helping God's men better understand **the new Man Code they are born into when they come to know and follow Jesus Christ.**

To be sure, shaking off the old code and putting on the new will mean that you have to spend a lot of time with Jesus. That means reading the Bible and praying—time well spent, we might add.

> **MARGINALIZED**: to put or keep someone in a powerless or unimportant position within a society or group.
>
> —*Merriam-Webster Dictionary*

God's plan is to transform you into His image through an intimate and abiding relationship with Jesus. That has always been God's plan. The Bible has a lot to say about abiding with Jesus, which is the same as spending time and connecting with Him.

Jesus illustrates the point to his disciples with a grapevine analogy in the Gospel of John when He said this:

> *"I am the vine; you are the branches. If you remain in me and I in you, you will bear much fruit; apart from me you can do nothing."*
>
> —JOHN 15:5, NIV

The apostle Paul built on this letting go of the old or culturally-influenced way of life in Ephesians 4:24 (NLT) when he wrote, "Put on your new nature, created to be like God—truly righteous and holy."

"This means that anyone who belongs to Christ becomes a new person," the Bible says in 2 Corinthians 5:17 (NLT). "The old life is gone; a new life has begun!"

TAKING NEW STEPS

Cracking the Man Code is about identifying the old Man Code way of life and taking bold steps towards becoming the new Man of God that He created you to be.

FROM THE TRIBE OF ISSACHAR, THERE WERE 200 LEADERS OF THE TRIBE WITH THEIR RELATIVES. ALL THESE MEN UNDERSTOOD THE SIGNS OF THE TIMES AND KNEW THE BEST COURSE FOR ISRAEL TO TAKE.

—1 CHRONICLES 12:32, NLT

In the following pages, we—pastor and educator Pete McKenzie and men's group leader Phil Van Horn—will teach and share first-person stories. Pete has devoted a lifetime to ministering to men as a principal of a Christian school, missionary to Eastern Europe, senior pastor of a Southern California church, and Western Director of Influencers West Men's Ministry in California. Phil is one of Pete's disciples, an Influencers West group leader, an Emmy Award-winning journalist, and a baseball and entertainment agent in Los Angeles.

Pete teaches that Jesus left His throne in heaven to rescue a world that was in crisis. That said, the world He entered over 2,000 years ago, based largely on political might and turmoil, was dramatically different from today.

Or was it?

Are men today that much different from the men of Jesus' day?

Perhaps not. The basic principles of human nature—sin, death, and judgment as well as righteousness, character, and faith—are as relevant to men today as they were to men in Jesus'

> **CRISIS**: a difficult or dangerous situation that needs serious attention; an unstable or crucial time or state of affairs in which a decisive change is impending; one with the distinct possibility of a highly undesirable outcome; a situation that has reached a critical phase.
>
> —*Merriam-Webster Dictionary*

time. We say that because we share the same struggles, issues, and problems regardless of culture.

At our core, God created all of us the same. When Jesus stepped into a time and place that was in crisis, political leaders violently opposed religious factions and yet created alliances with them for power and public opinion. Does this sound familiar to you?

In Jesus' time, the Roman Army occupied Israel and ruled with an iron fist. A succession of corrupt kings compounded the oppression. King

Herod, a tyrant, enriched himself and his friends and brutally repressed any threat. He slaughtered children by the hundreds to protect himself from the "Coming King of Israel." The identity of the much-prophesied "Coming King" was a mystery at the time.

> "WHEN THE CRISIS COMES AND COURAGE IS REQUIRED, GOD EXPECTS HIS MEN TO HAVE SUCH CONFIDENCE IN HIM THAT THEY WILL BE THE RELIABLE ONES."
>
> —OSWALD CHAMBERS, 19th century author of *My Utmost for His Highest*

Adding to the occupation by a Roman garrison was a corrupt and callous Jewish religious leadership called the Sanhedrin. Then there were the patriotic Jewish Zealots, who schemed to violently overthrow the regional Roman authority. The Zealots attempted to recruit Jesus as a warrior king to help their plan to free Israel from foreign occupation.

Jesus agreed he was a king during a poignant conversation with the Roman governor of Judea, Pontius Pilate, but he was not a king for warriors and patriots. "My kingdom is not of this world," he said in John 18:36 (NIV), just hours before his crucifixion, which Pilate authorized.

Jesus had a far different plan. To men steeped in Jewish culture and tradition, Jesus' teaching far exceeded their earthly understanding of day-to-day problems. Even today, men *still* struggle with this because men often focus on daily cultural traditions.

Jesus' new plan ran counter to the world's wisdom and ways. He proved just how different His plan was when he chose twelve rag-tag men who had no background or experience in leadership. His followers— the twelve disciples—were not educated to the world's path to success. They had a difficult time understanding and applying what Jesus lived and taught. That remains our problem today, trying to shed our old ways and understand Jesus' life and spirit.

A MINDSET OF CONFUSION

To further complicate things, there is nothing more spiritually damaging today than men who are professing Christians yet they do not really know Jesus. They do not understand Jesus' teaching, and as a result, they cannot reflect His true nature and character.

We realize that this is not a popular message, but far too many men today receive counsel from businessmen who apply competitive principles from work to church-going matters, rather than strong Christian believers who follow Jesus' teaching in all aspects of their lives—including important workplace matters.

Or as Pete likes to say, "Too many men listen to businessmen who happen to be Christians, instead of Christians who happen to be businessmen."

That same mindset confused and marginalized men of Jesus' day, including His disciples as well as the politicians, zealots, and religious leaders. Having been rejected by Jesus, those same leaders may have asked, "Okay, what is your plan?"

Jesus may have pointed to a tax collection booth set up in the marketplace and responded, "See that guy over there?"

"Yeah, that's Levi," fellow Jews would reply. "He's a traitor of the worst kind. He gouges us with extra taxes. He's cheating his own people and getting rich. We hate his guts." We're certain that Jesus could understand their disdain.

"That might be," Jesus would have nodded. "But he's part of the plan. And over there at the water's edge, see those fishermen mending their nets?"

"You mean the troublemakers James and John, the guys they call 'The Sons of Thunder,' and that big-mouth Peter?"

Any passerby would have expected Jesus to share their sentiment because they looked at them as fishermen who offended everyone with their swearing and stench.

Jesus likely would have answered again, "That might be. But they are part of the plan."

Jesus intentionally chose common, socially unimportant, and marginalized men to turn the world right-side up. He is still doing that today:

> *But God chose the foolish things of the world to shame the wise.*
>
> —1 Corinthians 1:26a, NIV

The apostle Paul wrote that. Jesus changed Saul of Tarsus from a rabbi who tortured Christians into a man who would author nearly half of the New Testament.

That shouldn't surprise us. **Jesus did big *uncommon* things with little *common* things.** He still does.

He called twelve common men to start an uncommon movement to change the world. Those men became what we now know as His disciples.

You see, **Jesus often prefers availability instead of capability,** or heartfelt humility rather than knowledge of church rules. The original twelve disciples are a good example.

We believe Jesus is still calling men today.

Perhaps He is calling *you* to start, grow, or renew a relationship with Him. It is important for a man who calls himself a follower of Christ to understand that he is part of the plan.

When a man feels unworthy, it's nearly impossible for him to know if he is part of the plan. But until you realize you are *not* unworthy in God's eyes, you will never be in God's plan as we are discussing here.

We know that men may not feel unworthy hanging out with other guys at work or on the golf course. But generally in their homes and in the church, men feel unworthy as defined here.

When Pete started trying to define a man of God, he was a Christian school principal in his hometown of Birmingham, Alabama.

The school had a great guy on their faculty named Jeff Young who had an annoying habit. Every time he would see Pete at school, he would point at him and say resolutely, "Man of God!"

Jeff's declaration always made Pete feel uncomfortable. He would usually look behind himself to see who Jeff was pointing at, only to find it was him. Pete figured he had at least one guy fooled.

> **UNWORTHY**: not good enough to deserve something or someone; not accepted, loved or approve of; lacking in excellence or value; worthless, base, poor; undeserving; inappropriate to one's condition or station; to be lacking; to not have enough to get the job done.
>
> —*Merriam-Webster Dictionary*

Why was Pete so uncomfortable? Why would any guy be?

Pete says he was uncomfortable because he had a wrong view of himself and a wrong view of God. He allowed his sin to turn to guilt and shame. He felt a constant intimidation, and the accusations from the devil all but paralyzed him spiritually. Those feelings stole the joy from his heart and had him spiritually running around in circles. He was a confused man.

When Pete became a pastor to men, he began to spend time asking God to help him understand what a Man of God really is.

What we are teaming up to share in *Cracking the Man Code* is that we're certainly not the last word on what defines a Man of God. But Pete's journey of understanding what a Man of God is has given him tremendous insights, and these days, Pete has the privilege of sharing his understanding of what God has shown him with thousands of men.

You are one of those persons. You, too, can become a Man of God.

Welcome to the journey.

1
AVERAGE, CASUAL PROBLEMS

The next time you're in church on a Sunday morning, take a look around you.

See the guys standing while the worship band plays on? They're just like you really—an average father, husband, or brother. In fact, the average guy in church is like the average guy everywhere. They share many things in common, including vulnerability, brokenness, jealousies, and strife.

This book describes the average guy in church and the struggles he faces. We will not only be taking a look at what he is like,

> **AVERAGE**: a level that is typical of a group, class, or series; a middle point between extremes.
>
> —*Merriam-Webster Dictionary*

but **we will also encourage the average guy to step out of a casual mindset to life and step into becoming a Man of God.** This often takes time and effort.

What we see from our time working with men is that the average guy in church has two common problems, and it's amazing how prevalent these problems are with all men.

One problem is his view of himself. The other is his view of God.

We want to help you see yourself not in light of today's culture but as God sees you. God is who He says He is and not who your friends and family or popular culture tell you who He is. If we can help you see God for who He *really* is, you won't fall for the deception and lies that this culture and the devil promote.

We hope that *Cracking the Man Code* will help you understand that

God—who has great compassion for His men—**chooses average guys to be part of His plan to reconcile a lost world to Himself**. In fact, **He wants to restore you and other men to their rightful place as men of God** for a time such as this.

So let Him choose you.

The apostle Paul said that the best servants of the Lord are those men who, in the world's eyes, are basically nothing and need to know their place. God most often works best with men who have been humbled and are willing to serve Him, which is why the following passage from Scripture is one of our favorites:

> *Remember, dear brothers and sisters, that few of you were wise in the world's eyes or powerful or wealthy when God called you. Instead, **God chose things the world considers foolish in order to shame those who think they are wise.** And he chose things that are powerless to shame those who are powerful. God chose things despised by the world, things counted as nothing at all, and used them to bring to nothing what the world considers important. As a result, no one can ever boast in the presence of God.*
>
> —1 Corinthians 26-29 (NLT),
> with boldface added for emphasis

Let God choose you, even if you feel unworthy. A man who knows he is foolish and weak, who knows he is not influential, mighty, or wise, a man who knows that's he not intellectually gifted can be used by God, even if that man feels unworthy because he lacks these worldly values.

Keep in mind that the man who finds his righteousness in Jesus is free and at peace. This man is strong, adequate, and secure. He has become a man of wisdom that is not his own. He possesses a power that he never had before, and he becomes a man the world desperately needs, but of whom the world is not worthy.

Don't be like other average men who believe their righteousness, or their right way of thinking, is more valuable and important than God's righteousness. They do not understand His righteousness can turn them from an average guy into a Man of God.

When God looks at any man, He does not see sin—He sees Jesus' righteousness in that man, which should have you shouting *Hallelujah!*

DON'T BECOME A CASUALTY

Since we're all average, it's likely that many of us have an average, even casual relationship with God.

That, guys, is a challenge, and here's why.

It's our contention that the casual guy in church is increasingly like the casual guy everywhere. The problem with that observation and our experience is that **casual Christian men will become *casualties* someday.**

The laws of spirit and nature have revealed that a casual approach to following Jesus Christ results in a man becoming a casualty of faith. When temptation abounds, problems arise.

> **CASUAL:** happening by chance, not by plan; designed for or permitting the ordinary; done without much thought, effort, or concern.
>
> —*Merriam-Webster Dictionary*

And people slowly drift away . . . casually.

Most men today are casual about their faith in God. For them, Sunday church is hit-or-miss. Reading the Bible rarely happens. They have an excuse for missing or totally avoiding men's group gatherings. **These men are on *their* plan**, not God's plan.

Sure, the demands of work and carving out family time apply pressure. There never seems to be enough room for genuine spiritual development. A healthy spiritual life requires discipline, sacrifice, and attention, and those attributes are in short supply.

George Barna, the founder of The Barna Group, a market research firm that studies the religious beliefs and behavior of Americans, began noticing an uptick in "casual attitudes" among Christians in the 1980s.

"Numerous indicators suggest that rather than adhering to a Christian philosophy of life that is occasionally tarnished by lapses into infidelity, **many Christians are profoundly secularized, and only occasionally do they respond to conditions and situations in a Christian manner,**" Barna wrote in his book, *Vital Signs: Emerging Social Trends and the Future of American Christianity*. "Recent research shows that many Christians are especially vulnerable to the worldly philosophies of materialism, humanism, and hedonism. Perhaps at no prior moment in history have so many Christians waged the battle for piety and holiness so casually and failed so consistently."

What's even more astonishing is that Barna penned these words in 1984! Nearly thirty-five years later, churches are *still* devoting much of their time to cleaning up the lives of men who are average or casual in their faith and suffering the consequences of their sin.

A CASUAL STANDARD

So who is the average man in church today? What are some typical characteristic traits? He is:

- ↗ insecure
- ↗ fearful
- ↗ stagnant

Which means he is also:

- ↗ inadequate
- ↗ isolated
- ↗ lonely

Just as he is casual relationally with Jesus, he is equally casual and distant with just about everybody including his wife, his children, his parents, and his siblings.

Since he generally feels under-challenged by his church, he is sure that he must look elsewhere to be a part of something bigger or more challenging. Often, it's his job or what he does to make money, but it can also be hobbies or following a sport. He has misplaced his priorities, but he rarely takes time to consider how to make things right.

He's too busy working hard and usually putting in more overtime than is either needed or healthy. He is stressed out and hates what his life has become but doesn't think he can do anything about it. He feels trapped and like he is running on empty. Emotional and physical exhaustion are his constant companions. It's entirely likely that his spiritual reserves are drained as well.

Under such a scenario, the temptation to make poor character decisions is common. Being tempted is not a sin, however. The problem is when you give in to sin. The best way to fight temptation is by staying in close proximity to Jesus, and that happens by spending time with Him in His Word and hanging around other believers.

In the midst of temptation, the average man has little or no hope that things can change. He has a hard time seeing Jesus as the source of hope.

Physically, the average guy does not take care of himself. And although he is aware of the importance of good health, he does not:

- ↗ exercise enough
- ↗ lose excess weight
- ↗ eat well
- ↗ sleep at least seven or eight hours a night
- ↗ see a doctor even when he suspects something is wrong

Spiritually and personally, he struggles with:

- ↗ guilt and shame
- ↗ believing God loves him
- ↗ receiving and giving grace, or understanding the biblical benefit or value of grace

- ↗ making and keeping commitments, regardless of importance, because he wants to "keep his options open"
- ↗ acting ethically in all facets of life
- ↗ planning for the future

He rarely says common yet very important and freeing phrases such as:

- ↗ "I am wrong."
- ↗ "I'm sorry" or "I apologize."
- ↗ "I do not know."
- ↗ "I'm hurting."
- ↗ "I need help."
- ↗ "I love you."

This was one of the easiest parts of the book for me (Phil) to write because I can't remember just once hearing my father say these things. My father was not alone. The inability to admit fault or be vulnerable stems from a deeply embedded cultural "Man Code" that has not served men well at all.

Here is *why* men refuse to say:

"I am wrong."

Because someone will think I'm weak.

"I'm sorry."

Because my pride gets in the way.

"I don't know."

Because I don't want others to think that I'm ignorant.

"I'm hurting."

Because I don't want others to think that I can't take it.

"I need help."

Because I don't want others to think I'm not capable.

"I love you."

Because I don't want to have to back it up, which can be costly.

These Man Code tendencies will always lead you to feel unworthy. This is part of the spiritual battle that you're fighting.

LET THE TRUTH SET YOU FREE

We're here to remind you that all guys face the same struggles, and that includes you. What you need is a reminder that there's freedom in Christ, and that comes from reading Jesus' words in John 8:32 (NLT), when He said, "Then you will know the truth, and the truth will set you free."

What does that look like?

The free man will say, "I'm wrong" and sincerely mean it.

The free man will say, "I'm sorry" and express a desire to make things right.

The free man will admit, "I don't know" and not feel shame.

The free man will share, "I am hurting" and not feel weak.

The free man will gently say, "I need help" and embrace being humble.

The free man will sincerely say, "I love you" and mean it.

When there's brokenness, there's freedom and peace. When pride is pushed aside, there's humility and honesty. You will feel closer to Jesus, who wants you to spend time and connect with Him.

God does not see flawed and sinful men as they are but as they will be. **What He's asking you to do is to give yourself in total abandonment and place your absolute trust in Him.**

We appreciate how The Message translation describes how the foolish become wise and the weak become strong when Jesus comes into their lives. Here are the Apostle Paul's words:

> Take a good look, friends, at who you were when you got called into this life. I don't see many of "the brightest and the best" among you, not many influential, not many from high-society families. Isn't it obvious that God deliberately chose men and

women that the culture overlooks and exploits and abuses, chose these "nobodies" to expose the hollow pretensions of the "somebodies"? That makes it quite clear that none of you can get by with blowing your own horn before God. Everything that we have—right thinking and right living, a clean slate and a fresh start—comes from God by way of Jesus Christ. That's why we have the saying, "If you're going to blow a horn, blow a trumpet for God."

—1 CORINTHIANS 1:26-31 (MSG)

Sound familiar? Yep, that's a different translation of the same Scripture we used earlier in this chapter.

Now, we would like you to consider these verses:

It is by grace you have been saved, through faith—and this is not from yourselves, it is the gift of God— not by works, so that no one can boast.

—EPHESIANS 2:8-9 (NIV)

I have been crucified with Christ and I no longer live, but Christ lives in me. The life I now live in the body, I live by faith in the Son of God, who loved me and gave himself for me.

—GALATIANS 2:20 (NIV)

The Bible verses are all talking about one thing: **change that occurs in a man's life happens when he encounters Jesus Christ.**

In today's culture, change is needed, which is why we will explore two areas of challenge in the next chapter. These problems, which have tempted and hurt men throughout time, are often the main culprits in why men feel insecure, fearful, inadequate, isolated, and lonely.

DISCUSSION STARTER QUESTIONS

> Are you surprised to learn average guys in church are much like guys who don't attend church? What types of "casual" behavior do you see around your church?

> If worldly philosophies are materialism, humanism, and hedonism, what are opposite Christian ideals?

> What does it mean to be under-challenged at church? Cite an example on TV shows or commercials of an organization that challenges men to be part of something greater.

> *I'm wrong. I'm sorry. I need help. I love you.* What first thought popped into your mind as you read this list?

> The Bible says that not many of the best and brightest or influential people were among early believers. How does that align with the public perception of Christians today?

PETE'S PRAYER

Heavenly Father, this sounds like me. And I know it doesn't please You. I ask You to change my casual heart and make me the Man of God that You created me to be. Amen.

2
FATHER WOUND

As you just read, the name of this chapter is Father Wound. Now we'd like you to read the title of this chapter out loud and pause between each word:

Father. Wound.

The reason we're emphasizing a simple chapter title is because **the average man in the average church has a Father Wound.** Perhaps one that is deep and life-impacting.

Think about your father. What's the first thing you recall when your father comes to mind? Is it positive or negative? Did he treat you well or poorly? Was he loving, distant, or deranged? Did you see him all the time growing up or was he out of the picture? Or something in between?

While a few men have great fathers and great memories of growing up with their dads, the average guy has a deep and seemingly incurable Father Wound.

There's help for that profound pain, but many men don't know how or who to ask for help.

The Father Wound manifests itself in a variety of unhealthy ways throughout the stages of a man's life. The lingering emotional hurts can cause damaging thoughts and actions at key times—from interactions in the workplace to managing money to navigating marriage to raising children.

> **WOUND:** an injury to the body (as from violence, accident, or surgery); a mental or emotional hurt or blow.
>
> *—Merriam-Webster Dictionary*

Here's what Pete has to say about the stages of a Father Wound:

It's amazing how common it is for men to have Father Wounds, and I say that with confidence because I've listened to many men share their personal Father Wounds over the years.

Whenever we have a retreat, you should hear the groans that fill the auditorium when we ask men to gather in small groups and take two minutes to talk about the impact their fathers had on their lives. The grumbling happens nearly every time, which tells me that Father Wounds are painful and last for many years.

Men don't want to talk about their fathers. They are still hurting and even angry at their dads years later. Many believe they are going through life alone in their suffering. They can't put their fingers on exactly *why* they feel that way, but they just know that they've been emotionally and even physically hurt by their fathers.

It's not my intention to pile on or resurrect painful feelings that you could be harboring about your relationship with your father. What I want to do is put this topic on the table, get it out in the open, and ask you to take it to Jesus so that you can start healing. **Our Lord and Savior *wants* you to bring your Father Wound to Him.** Let Him be your Father.

If you're harboring resentment or a grudge toward your earthly father, then it would be instructive to understand the four stages of a Father Wound:

The Four Stages of a Father Wound

Stage 1: Introduction

The first stage is when young men begin to see or define what a man is about. The introduction or initial awareness of an impactful father, uncle, or adult male role model often begins between the ages of three to six.

Stage 2: Competition

Boys find out early on that to be successful they must compete and compete well. Not only must they contend with their siblings for parental attention and love, but they must compete at school for academic achievement and on the playing field for athletic glory. During adolescence and the young adult years, this competition evolves into attracting the attention of the opposite sex as well as their bosses in the race for promotions and pay increases.

Competition produces winners and losers. When one man succeeds, another one fails or falls behind.

Men fear failure just about more than anything.

Stage 3: Wounded

In a fallen world, suffering is common. Any soldier on the battlefield or any striving athlete in the arena of competition knows that he risks being wounded or getting hurt.

Wounds come in all forms. They can be deep and penetrating, as in an internal wound, or they can be on the surface as an external wound. The kind of wounds that we're talking about are deep and painful Father Wounds, which are internal but can come from physical abuse as well.

Stage 4: Healing

The final stage is the process for healing from a Father Wound. Unfortunately, most men never reach this stage. They remain stuck in the painful wounded stage and stay there for many years.

My Father Wound

My father took out his anger on the world on me (Phil) in horribly abusive ways. Among my earliest memories are getting spanked hard by my father, who used his bare hand on my bare bottom.

By the time I turned five, he was using leather belts and switches made from a thin tree limb to spank me. When he tired of that, he started swatting my bottom with electrical wires.

Each spanking, he said, was to teach me "right from wrong," but I always thought he was looking for an excuse to find something wrong. By the time I was eight, my spankings graduated into over-the-top whippings that rarely stopped until he physically exhausted himself.

The frequent red welts and occasional blood on my body didn't mean much to him. In fact, most of the whippings really had no meaning at all. Sure, I made mistakes. But to him, my little but poor decisions were equal to big, big problems. I also got whipped when I had done nothing wrong and he had a bad day, like receiving a speeding ticket at the local speed trap one day.

From age three to sixteen, I was whupped an average of once a month. There was rarely extended peace in our suburban Midwestern home.

I suppose him taking it out on me was his way of lashing back at the world around him. I really don't know to this day why my father unleashed his anger so consistently and vengefully on the youngest of three sons and a daughter. Not that he didn't attack them, too. I saw him brutalize my siblings with my own eyes, and I hurt for them when I recall those violent, ugly times. But it became obvious that he saved his most consistent and brutal punishment for me.

Why? Because I was convenient. I was the youngest and smallest. As my older brothers and sister graduated from high school and moved away, I was still there and in many ways left to fend for myself.

I'll never forget the time when my father literally sliced up my hands on a Saturday morning during my junior year of high school. In a rage, he intentionally jabbed a battery-powered grass-trimmer into the fingers on my left hand while it was on. Thank goodness the trimmer was clogged with thick grass, but the metal edges still sliced and peeled away my skin, causing bright red blood to gush out. Bare bones and knuckles were visible.

I had a baseball game that afternoon. Even though my still throbbing hand did not fit well into my baseball glove, I still wanted to play. Imagine trying to catch a baseball with multiple open cuts on your glove hand, and not one of them stitched up. When it was apparent that I couldn't catch a ball without experiencing great pain, I told my coaches I couldn't play and hid behind some excuse.

About a decade later, I started wondering if my father was a victim of childhood abuse. I discreetly asked my relatives about my father's upbringing. I learned that his parents worked him hard growing up. From an early age, he arose before dawn to perform chores on their 300-acre farm in Ohio. As was customary for the time, his parents spanked him for not doing what they wanted, but there was no evidence to indicate why he would take things up a notch and channel a high level of hatred and violence toward me.

One time, I finally pushed back.

I was standing in front of our two-car garage one day when my father rushed me in typical anger. I was sixteen years old at the time, not quite physically mature, but he was still beating me, usually inside the garage. This time, I stood up for myself.

I pushed him back on his chest and forced him away from me, even though he was much stronger than me.

"I love you, but it's time to stop the beatings—now!" I screamed.

It worked. He stepped back, likely out of shock.

After high school graduation, I left for college. My father had often told me during my teen years he didn't love me and wanted me to leave home. Leaving for college was a relief for both of us.

Yet the intense physical child abuse left more than scars on my skin. Any self-esteem I derived as a young adult came from sports and work. I struggled to relate to adult men. I resented their shortcomings. No forgiveness. No way.

When I was twenty years old, I visited his apartment. He was out of our home by then because my mother had rightfully divorced him. Our visit did not go well. In a flash, his volcano-like anger erupted at me. Out of nowhere, he pulled out a handgun and rushed me. My heart was in my throat when he pressed the tip of the gun on my chest.

"I ought to kill you and end it all!" he screamed.

I was too stunned to say anything or react. I just stared at the barrel of the pistol. But then he backed off. Perhaps he was in shock too.

Six years after sticking a gun in my chest, my father did not attend my wedding. I was in so much love and my bride, Lecia, looked so beautiful that I hardly noticed his absence. At the time, I was twenty-six years old, ten years removed from pushing back and six years removed from his gun in my chest. The scars I carried impacted my view of a loving Heavenly Father.

As I settled into marriage, having no father in my life was normal. Who wanted that madness anyway? Having any sort of relationship with my father would have made things worse, but as I stayed away from him, that created a divide between me and my mother, my sister, and my two brothers. I sought out ways to medicate myself to cope. Shame and guilt regularly accompanied my life's journey.

I just wanted the pain and negative impact on my life to stop, and I could not do it myself. Lord knows, I tried. I researched surviving child abuse and prayed often for God to help me heal and forgive, but I thought the pain and impact would never stop. There was no willing it away. I could not do it myself.

I tried out ideas from recovery programs and began reading the Bible. Over time and with trial and error, I learned to forgive and forgive again and keep forgiving, both my father and myself. I turned to my Heavenly Father. I asked Him for help.

I'm pleased to report that God helped me forgive my father whenever the pain surfaced, and He provided a level of His love to exceed the level of pain I felt. He still does.

I learned that it takes courage to repeatedly and knowingly visit personal darkness, to forgive and to heal, and to turn away in peace. I know men—tough men—who cannot do it. I understand. I could not do it without God. I'm not that strong.

I learned to consider that I am never completely healed. Instead, I am *in recovery* one day at a time. I am involved in a daily battle, and frequently my days are not easy.

An image on TV or perhaps a casual comment in conversation can rekindle an unpleasant memory. When that happens, I relive a beating and the senselessness of it all. (Believe me, it didn't take much to vividly recall trying to fit my sliced-up fingers in that baseball glove.) So, I forgive my father again, and the strength and courage to do so comes from God. That is the only way I can explain it.

I can tell you something else that helped: reading my Bible in a way that I had not previously. I've become hungry for God's Word. From my Bible and the Influencer's Ministry *Journey with Jesus*, I read that God wants to be my father and we are adopted into His family when we accept Him into our lives.

And that's exactly what I've done—praying and asking Him to be my Father, and He has answered that prayer and welcomed me as one of His sons.

These days, my children are in their twenties. They have never met my father. I have called him several times over the years, mostly on holidays, but the last time I called a decade ago he did not recognize my voice. When I told him who I was, he angrily slammed down the phone.

I still love him. I really do. And I forgive him, which must sound odd. So how did I get from a child-abuse victim to a forgiving adult? There is only one answer.

Jesus.

WHERE TO START THE HEALING

Many emotionally hurting men don't want to revisit their past or think about what it was like growing up with or without their fathers. Even if they are willing to face the present, they are unsure about how to start the healing process. So they go through life allowing this gaping wound to impact nearly every area of their existence.

Here are examples of how a Father Wound starts and grows. For example, you might have:

- grown up without a father in the home and have been looking all your life to fill the hole that no human dad can fill.

- grown up with an emotionally absent father who was home but never cared for you or spent much time with you.

- grown up with a harmful, verbally abusive father who said things about you that you still haven't forgotten years later.

- grown up with a physically abusive father who inflicted frequent and excessive physical punishment, including beatings that left physical as well as emotional scars.

- never grown up with the benefit of loving correction and believe that your father didn't care enough to discipline you.

- seen your father repeatedly lie, cheat, and steal.

- never received any kind of positive moral or spiritual mentoring.

- never once heard your father say, "I love you," or had a meaningful conversation about things that matter.

- never had father-son time ranging from something as simple as changing a bike tire to going on a weekend campout.

- never felt like you could please your father or be good enough for him.

- had a hard time respecting your father, which led to times of hating him and leaving behind self-inflicted wounds that haven't healed.

- ↗ seen your father mistreat your mom and witnessed sickening physical abuse.

- ↗ seen your mom verbally abuse or dominate your father, which caused you to lose respect for your dad.

All of these bullet points (and there are more) are ways men can be deeply wounded by fathers who themselves were possibly wounded in the same way.

We understand that too many dads today have grown up with fathers who didn't receive any spiritual mentoring in their younger years or develop the habits of attending church regularly, reading their Bibles, or praying. It's entirely possible that your father may lack awareness of even the most modest benefits and blessings of developing a relationship with Jesus.

This is where you can receive help because our Heavenly Father desires a personal and loving Father-son relationship with you and wants to heal you of all wounds.

Jesus talked directly to men who were wounded and tired of life's exhausting battles. You can lean your shoulder on Him. He's capable of healing that Father Wound: "He heals the brokenhearted and binds up their wounds," says Psalm 147:3 (NIV).

Tell Him what's hurting. Describe your feelings of anguish about your father—feelings that perhaps you've never voiced to anybody. Let Him apply a soothing balm to your wounds.

THE SPIRIT OF ADOPTION

God wants to adopt you as one of his Sons. Let Him become your father. He wants you to call Him "Abba," the Aramaic term for *father* but often interpreted as *Papa* or *Daddy* because of its deeply intimate, childlike meaning. Jesus used the term Abba once in the Gospel of Mark, and Paul used it twice in his epistles to the Romans and the Galatians.

One of the Holy Spirit's names is the "Spirit of Adoption." We know this because Romans 8:15 (ESV) says, "For you did not receive the spirit of slavery to fall back into fear, but you have received the Spirit of adoption as sons, by whom we cry, 'Abba! Father!'"

Our God in heaven is called a "father to the fatherless" in Psalm 68:5. In Romans 8:23 (NLT), we learn this: "And we believers also groan, even though we have the Holy Spirit within us as a foretaste of future glory, for we long for our bodies to be released from sin and suffering. We, too, wait with eager hope for the day when God will give us our full rights as his adopted children, including the new bodies he has promised us."

Even if you've carelessly walked away from your Father in heaven in the past, He's willing to wrap His arms around your shoulders today. All you have to do is take a step toward Him.

For some, that first step can be the longest, but once you turn in His direction, you will have a totally different view of Him. Once you embrace His love, you will talk about what a wonderful Father He is.

CHANGE CAN HAPPEN NOW

One of the more common reasons why men don't want to take a step toward their Heavenly Father stems from the absence of spiritual mentoring.

It's been our experience that many men today are two to three generations removed from any form of church attendance, Bible reading, and prayer. **Yet reading the Bible with other men and praying out loud with them, while initially awkward, is powerful.** If that's your situation, then know that you can change right now.

Healing from deep wounds will require you to adjust your image of who God is. We begin by stating that the Creator of the Universe desires a loving Father-son relationship with you. That is who God is—the ultimate perfect Father.

Only our Heavenly Father can heal the Father Wounds that we've described. He gives us guidance through His Word, that, if embraced, can heal every wound.

Here's a list—by no means complete—of Father Wounds followed by a healing Scripture:

If you grew up without a dad and are still searching . . .

"And I will be your Father, and you will be
my sons and daughters, says the Lord Almighty."
2 CORINTHIANS 6:18, NLT

For God has said, "I will never
fail you. I will never abandon you."
HEBREWS 13:5B, NLT

If you're longing to see your father or have a relationship with him . . .

Then Jesus said, "Come to me, all of
you who are weary and carry heavy
burdens, and I will give you rest."
MATTHEW 11:28, NLT

If you grew up with an absentee father . . .

A father to the fatherless . . .
is God in his holy dwelling.
PSALM 68:5, NIV

If you grew up with a stranger you called Dad . . .

You made me; you created me. Now give me
the sense to follow your commands.
PSALM 119:73, NLT

If you heard constant criticism . . .

He heals the brokenhearted
and binds up their wounds.
PSALM 147:3, NIV

If you had a hard time respecting your father . . .

"For if you forgive other people when they sin against
you, your heavenly Father will also forgive you."
MATTHEW 6:14, NIV

If you grew up with a lying, cheating, and stealing father . . .

The fear of the Lord is the beginning of knowledge,
but fools despise wisdom and instruction.
PROVERBS 1:7, NIV

*If you grew up two to three generations removed from spiritual
mentoring . . .*

And let us not neglect our meeting together,
as some people do, but encourage one another . . .
HEBREWS 10:25A, NLT

*If you grew up with a father who lacked discipline and didn't
care about you . . .*

. . . don't make light of the Lord's discipline,
and don't give up when he corrects you. For the
Lord disciplines those he loves, and he punishes
each one he accepts as his child.
HEBREWS 12:5-6, NLT

If you grew up with a father who physically abused you . . .

The Lord replies, "I have seen violence done
to the helpless . . . I will rise up to rescue them,
as they have longed for me to do."
PSALM 12:5, NLT

"TO FORGIVE IS TO SET A PRISONER FREE
AND DISCOVER THAT THE PRISONER WAS YOU."

—LEWIS B. SMEDES, theologian and author

If you grew up with a great father, with few wounds if any, take time now to thank God for your dad. And you young dads, pray that you could be a dad as great to your kids as your father was to you.

If you were a physically abused child and the pain is unresolved, however, please seek help. It's never too late. Start now. Meet and pray with your pastor. Find a Christian counselor with a family practice. Start and finish counseling sessions with prayer.

Ask God for the courage to face unresolved pain and take steps toward healing. Don't expect a one-time super-healing. Instead, continue to trust God. Forgive, and forgive again.

DISCUSSION STARTER QUESTIONS

> Where in this chapter did your thoughts drift from reading to a painful incident with your father? Or at which age did you become aware of your father's most destructive (or helpful) habits?

> Which Father Wound paired with healing Scripture helped you the most?

> Who or what in your life do you need to forgive, perhaps break a destructive cycle and stop poisoning yourself?

> How can you start reading the Bible out loud and praying with one other guy or a small group of trusted men?

Action point: You can contact Bill Kauble at bkauble@InfluencersWest. org and order copies of *Journey with Jesus* for your small group or Bible study.

PETE'S PRAYER

Father, you teach us to forgive and that we must forgive to be forgiven. We trust You and agree. Show us how to forgive our dads for those of us who need that. Lord, help me to read Your Word and pray with my wife or a friend. In Jesus' name, amen.

3
SEX, MARRIAGE, AND SEXUAL INTEGRITY

Sex, outside of the purposes for how God created it, is a problem. There doesn't seem to be much sexual integrity in this world, which is about honesty and purity within a marriage relationship.

God brought two together, a man and woman, a husband and wife, to become one flesh. That means one flesh physically, emotionally, and spiritually. They are all tied together—especially for women. Guys tend to be hardwired for the physical part.

We feel strongly that the health of a marriage can often be judged by the condition of a married couple's sexual life. If the marriage is growing, stable, and strong, there is usually healthy sex in the relationship. If the marriage is struggling, however, problems in the bedroom can drastically impact the relationship.

From what we've seen with the Influencer's ministry, we can confidently state that when the average Christian man struggles in his marriage, usually the big reason is the lack of a vibrant sexual relationship with his wife, which leads to issues of sexual integrity.

This happens for several reasons. For instance, he is not as interested in marriage as his wife, who likely had been dreaming of her wedding day and thinking about what it would be like to be married all of her life. When you add the different expectations that both sides have regarding sex in the marriage, small problems can crop up in their relationship.

While marriage may define her, this is different from how he sees himself. He probably didn't start thinking about being married until a couple of months before the actual event. This simplistically explains why the differing expectations have dramatic implications for their sexual relationship as well as the future of their union.

It's also our experience that many men received no marriage preparation, didn't attend any premarital classes, haven't read any books on being married, or haven't received Christian premarital counseling (which we strongly recommend). That means he is unprepared for the demands that marriage requires or the changes in his personal life.

Throughout the years, God has given me (Pete) the opportunity to be in ministry with men and couples as well as the gift of being allowed to watch two of the most wonderful sights and movements of the Holy Spirit.

With couples, this happens when I teach them about the "prayer hug"—a time when a man will hold his wife and pray with her and over her. When he's finished, I can hear chains falling off all over the room.

I love the looks on the wives' faces. This is a moment they've longed to have with their husbands, sharing this kind of intimate prayer with their husbands. When the chains fall off, tears of joy spring forth, mostly from wives but from many husbands as well.

IN THE SAME WAY, YOU HUSBANDS MUST GIVE HONOR TO YOUR WIVES. TREAT YOUR WIFE WITH UNDERSTANDING AS YOU LIVE TOGETHER. SHE MAY BE WEAKER THAN YOU ARE, BUT SHE IS YOUR EQUAL PARTNER IN GOD'S GIFT OF NEW LIFE. TREAT HER AS YOU SHOULD SO YOUR PRAYERS WILL NOT BE HINDERED.

—1 PETER 3:7 (NLT)

I find that many husbands *want* to pray with their wives, but there's a spiritual barrier between the couple that the man does not know how to get through. Often the insecurity of not really knowing how to pray and being uncomfortable on that turf becomes an issue, especially with her. Or, it may be unresolved conflict between him and his wife. I can assure you that unresolved conflict—between us and God, and us and our mates—will be a barrier to prayer every time.

Why would you seek to have an intimate moment with someone you are at odds with? Most men are hamstrung by the barriers created by both God and wives, thinking that neither one of them is pleased with him. When that happens, he has to fight through this way of thinking and not allow the devil's lies to influence him. He must not allow his guilt, shame, and fear to win this battle. Too much is at stake.

Fight through it, men! Do it anyway! God will meet you where you are and do amazing things. Give Him something to work with. He will do His part if you will do yours.

Yes, it will take faith and courage. But remember this from Oswald Chambers, author of *My Utmost for His Highest*: "When the crisis comes and courage is required, God expects His men to have such confidence in Him that they will be the dependable ones."

PRAYER WORKS IN A MARRIAGE

When it comes to intimacy with your wife, keep these thoughts in mind:

- ↗ Be aware of the benefit when you consistently pray with your spouse.

- ↗ Prayer in all aspects of life provides strength, wisdom, and guidance. Add to that protection from attack by the devil. Prayer connects the heart and mind of men to God's heart and mind and places marriage and family under the umbrella of His protection.

- ↗ The opposite of two joined consistently in prayer is isolation, which often leads to destruction in relationships.

↗ God makes Himself available to be your refuge and hope. Lack of prayer leaves you to your own wisdom in a fierce spiritual struggle against the world, the flesh, and the devil.

↗ When you feel that you cannot please her, she will often not accept you for who you are. That's when you feel like you cannot be yourself and still be loved. Sure, you know that you're not perfect, but you will resent repeated attempts from her to change or "improve" you.

↗ Keep in mind that women are 25,000-words-a-day people and men speak half as much, around 12,000 words a day. Many women define intimacy often by access to daily details in a man's life and are interested in every aspect of their husband's life. Men commonly communicate in unspoken terms and cannot recall daily details.

↗ Of course, you would like her to be as interested in having sex as you are. Some wives actually may have equal or regular interest in sex, but the communication gap creates different languages or expectations of the joy of sex within marriage. For some wives, sex is part of the total relationship between her and her husband, so sex for her is a bonus to an emotional and intimate relationship with him. Also, wives may want to know if they can have an honest and intimate relationship without every meaningful encounter ending in sex.

Because of those challenges:

1. **He does not initiate date nights, doing a hobby or a sport together, or even romantic weekend getaways** (that we call "mini-moons") for those who have the time and resources to get away. These are examples of a man focusing solely on his wife and each other, which can be uncommon for a man but are remarkably important for women.

"Time together" tells her in direct terms that she is his focus regardless of surrounding circumstances. I recommend a long weekend getaway of three days and two nights away from home, just to focus on their relationship. Consider the likely positive impact a long weekend would have on your relationship if you were able to get away twice a year.

2. **He does not go to counseling for himself or his marriage.** In the old Man Code, going to counseling means, "I cannot handle it myself." Men also keep their problems a secret, which rules out counseling. Many women are the opposite and have no such inhibitions. Asking for help is logical and makes sense to them, while men tend not to see the problems in their relationship as many women do.

When a man is resistant to counseling, it says to his wife he does not care about her and their marriage. This attitude also explains why he is not as interested in anything designed to work on his marriage such as couples' retreats, workshops, Sunday school classes, and reading something that improves marriage and relationships.

Those are a few thoughts regarding communication, emotional intimacy, and sex between a husband and wife.

AFFAIRS IN A MARRIAGE

What about sex outside of marriage?

This issue must be addressed; it would be foolhardy to dismiss the topic of extramarital affairs. As many as 35 percent of Christian men cheat on their spouses according to research conducted by the Barna Group and Proven Men Ministries, a biblically based organization committed to serving and healing men suffering from sexual sin.

There's no wiggle room when it comes to extramarital affairs. God made it clear in the Ten Commandments when He declared, "Thou shall not commit adultery."

WHAT THE BIBLE HAS TO SAY ABOUT EXTRAMARITAL AFFAIRS

"You shall not commit adultery."
EXODUS 20:14 AND DEUTERONOMY 5:18, NIV

... do not be unfaithful to the wife of your youth.
MALACHI 2:15c, NIV

"You have heard that it was said,
'You shall not commit adultery.' "
MATTHEW 5:27
This commandment is repeated in the
Book of Romans and the Book of James

God designed sex for a husband and wife to express their deep love for each other. God wants to bless sex between a husband and wife. But He wants us to have sex within the guidelines He set for us. He does not want us to have sex with someone who is not our spouse.

Sexual integrity is honesty and purity about sex between a husband and wife. Lacking sexual integrity is all that happens outside of that definition. The lack of sexual integrity is often a problem today for individuals and society as a whole, for believers and non-believers alike.

We've witnessed an explosion of sexual harassment scandals that have cost powerful—and predatory—men their jobs and their stature in today's culture. From major media figures like Harvey Weinstein and Matt Lauer to political figures on both sides of the aisle in the nation's capital, it seems like there's always someone in the news being accused of using their position to demand sexual favors of a woman trying to break into Hollywood or move up the political or corporate ladder. And social media is filled with #MeToo postings.

The popular culture may try to spin this as a sex, porn, or men-behaving-badly problem, but Pete says this explosion of sexual harassment is a sin problem.

And the only way to deal with a sin problem is by pointing out that the only true solution to overcoming sexual sin is by having an abiding love, respect, and devotion to Jesus. When hearts are fixed on Him and eyes are fixed on His teachings—such as treating others as you would have them treat you—then lives are transformed and women receive respect and proper treatment in the workplace and in social settings. Pete has always said that if you want to change a culture, just be a committed, devoted Christian and *act like it!*

The miracle of it all is that we have a God who has invited us to repent and turn to Him and that He would forgive our sins and heal us. This is a universal promise to everyone, even Misters Weinstein and Lauer, and the thousands of men who are guilty of these same sins.

This is an area where you want to walk the straight and narrow regarding your interactions with women in the workplace and how you treat women in general and your wife in particular. Regarding the latter, take the steps necessary—by investing in romance and "our time"—so that the two of you don't become isolated or tempted to have sex outside of marriage or get caught up in the snare of pornography.

IT'S A BIG PROBLEM

Porn is a huge deal in the Church.

The same research performed by the Barna Group and Proven Men Ministries revealed that 55 percent of Christian men look at pornography at least once a month. The number is higher for Christian men between the ages of eighteen and thirty: 77 percent view pornography at least monthly and 36 percent look at pictures and videos of naked women at least once a day.

There's no way to avoid the fact that porn is a big problem inside the Church and traps pastors as well. Best-selling author and pastor Chuck Swindoll said that porn is the "number-one secret problem in the church. It's ruining marriages, destroying relationships, harming youth, and hurting the body of Christ."

What porn does to a marriage is that viewing these images of "porn queens" reduces a man's sexual interest in his wife. Often, she can't compete with the women featured in porn in terms of their bodies or what they are willing to do.

Because of the porn "baggage" often brought into marriage, it's possible the average Christian man doesn't know what a healthy sexual relationship looks like or what the phrase "sexual integrity" means. He may think porn isn't that big a deal because he's seen so much of it and is even unaware that he can lose his job if he's caught watching porn at work.

For men, watching porn either slightly undermines or completely destroys healthy sexual intimacy with his wife as well as any form of moral authority with family, friends, and community.

The last point is worth talking about. Men often shy away from expressing biblical truths when they are hiding a secret themselves. **Porn takes a man off the spiritual playing field probably more than any other sin.** They aren't as likely to serve in the church or step into any sort of leadership role because they have this thing—addiction, really—for looking at porn.

This type of sexual sin can be devastating in many ways.

Dr. John MacArthur, president of the Master's University and pastor of Grace Community Church in Los Angeles, said, "There is a sense in which sexual sin destroys a person like no other because it is so intimate and entangling, corrupting on the deepest human level. No sin has greater potential to destroy the body."

God's Word warns us in 1 Corinthians 6:18-20 (NLT):

Run from sexual sin! No other sin so clearly affects the body as this one does. For sexual immorality is a sin against your own body. Don't you realize that your body is the temple of the Holy Spirit, who lives in you and was given to you by God? You do not belong to yourself, for God bought you with a high price. So, you must honor God with your body.

When there is sin, it weakens the entire body of Christ.

Most people may not understand that spiritual warfare is constant in a fallen world. Given that battle, porn is not the issue. Pornography is a means to an end for the devil, a tool in his hand to steal the soul of a man of God and greatly damage his relationship with God and Christ. The devil wants to neutralize God's leaders and everyday good men, and keep them from having the impact and power to change a culture as God created them to do.

BREAKING THE CHAINS

Perhaps you have a problem with porn. God knows your actions, and He knows your heart.

If you're drawn to porn sites and raunchy videos, the first thing we want to say is that you are not alone. Porn is amazingly addictive *and* progressive. The pleasure jolt you receive from consuming porn has you coming back for more.

From what we've seen at the Influencer's ministry, we understand why men naturally fear being found out and connected to porn. This explains why ministering to men about porn is often a challenge. Because of guilt and shame, men don't want to be ministered to—or ask for help to break an addiction to porn.

But this is the time to ask for help.

How do you break an addiction to porn and overall deal with sin and the consequences of sin?

You start with Jesus. We tell men that the comeback road begins with reading Matthew 11:28 (NLT), in which Jesus said, "Come to me all of you who are weary and carry heavy burdens, and I will give you rest."

Spiritually, this means spending time with Jesus through reading His Word. **A good habit to start is reading passages of Scripture before work and again, if only briefly at night, before you fall asleep.** You will be surprised at the positive impact that a dose of Jesus Christ can do to transform a mind.

Another way to spend time with Jesus is to listen on the car radio to sermons and worship music during your daily commute. You can listen to Christian content on your smartphone while you run or work out.

This is also the time to ask God to remove your appetite for porn. Instead, replace that with a new appetite for that which is fulfilling—Jesus Christ.

As Pete has said over the years, "Hang out at His screen door. You'll be glad you did."

DISCUSSION STARTER QUESTIONS

> Have you gone through Christian premarital counseling? What was that like? How did your fiancée or wife react to it? What are the possible benefits?

> Can you imagine starting the day with a "prayer hug"? How do you think your wife would react?

> What are the benefits of praying together with your wife or girl-friend? Why is fighting isolation important?

> How do you fight or reject the presence of porn, nudity, or sexual imagery in the mass media (ads, movies, TV shows)? If you're losing the battle of sexual integrity, we recommend the book *Every Man's Battle*, which teaches you to identify problem circumstances and how to "bounce your eyes" whenever you see a scantily dressed woman.

> A Man Code challenge: Read one Bible verse or chapter in the morning. For the last thing at night, read one more verse or chapter and then pray with your wife. Start today. Stay with this practice, even though you may forget or miss a day.

> What is the easiest or simplest way for you to use your smartphone to "hang out" with Jesus and practice sexual integrity? Would it be listening to Christian music or sermons? Could you listen to worship music on an app?

PETE'S PRAYER

Father, I am a man. I struggle with sexual temptation every day of my life—it's that powerful and present all around me. I ask You to help me love You so much that my desire for holiness and purity causes me to be offended rather than tempted by sexual temptation.

4
REACHING A SPIRITUAL PLATEAU

The average Christian man in the average church often feels like he has reached a spiritual plateau.

When he stands on the plateau, he's not changing for good or for bad. There's no progress. And if there's no progress, the reality is that he's moving backwards. **His casual spirituality is hurting him.** He is in danger of becoming a spiritual casualty.

He may express public pride about his faith, but that is often a false pride. He knows in his heart something big is missing.

> **PLATEAU**: a relatively stable, level, period or condition; a level of attainment or achievement.
>
> —*Merriam-Webster Dictionary*

A man will know he has reached a spiritual plateau when he admits he listens to sermons with "one ear" or lets **the pastor's words go "in one ear and out the other."** This is the textbook definition of the casual approach to a relationship with God.

A man will know that he has reached his spiritual plateau when he stops attending men's retreats, Bible studies, Sunday school classes, or large stadium events like Greg Laurie's Harvest America because of his half-hearted approach.

A man will know that he has reached his spiritual plateau when he becomes one of these "not enough" Christian guys. Sure, he attends church services and reads his Bible every now and then, but he knows that's "not enough."

Because of his casual relationship with God, he knows there's a lot more to having a personal relationship with Christ, but he's not there yet and knows it. If asked to speak honestly, he would say his relationship with Jesus isn't his highest priority. If asked why, he responds with a dumbfounded look. The cares of the world and the desires for riches have choked his appetite for God's Word.

A man will know that he has reached his spiritual plateau when he senses that he needs an accountability group, but he doesn't make a move to join one or says the ones he's attended in the past didn't help that much.

MINISTERING TO MEN

When a man joins an accountability group, one of three things will happen:

1. He will be honest and share struggles.

2. He will be dishonest and hide his struggles.

3. He will not show up because he knows he will be asked hard questions that he has no intention of answering.

A man will know that he has reached his spiritual plateau when he struggles with transparency and vulnerability. In these situations, he often feels like throwing in the towel spiritually because **he just cannot seem to be the "good Christian" he is supposed to be and mistakenly perceives other men to be.**

In Pete's experience, men who think this way have never been able to shake their works-based understanding of God's blessing and salvation. They have heard that God is gracious to sinners, but they feel that's what happens to other sinners and not them. They have never embraced the grace of God or the unmerited favor given by Him and feel they don't deserve His forgiveness. That leads to a lot of self-loathing because they feel unworthy.

If that's your situation, think about this Scripture:

> *God saved you by his grace when you believed. And you cannot take credit for this; it is a gift from God. Salvation is not a reward for the good things we have done, so none of us can boast about it.*
>
> —EPHESIANS 2:8-9 (NLT)

God saves us because He loves us. **Grace is His idea and His gift to us. He does all of the work. We do not save ourselves.** If we did, we would likely take credit for it. And then we would lose that special Father-child relationship with Him.

A man's pride in the Man Code says he must earn something in order to receive it. Receiving something he has *not* earned seems like a handout. He is desperately fearful of what others think about him. It's a wonderful day, though, when a man breaks through his need to work for his salvation as well as his acceptance from God. When he realizes he does not deserve and cannot earn his salvation and blessing from God, he makes peace with a wonderful spiritual reality.

LIVING RIGHT BEFORE GOD

A man will know that he has reached his spiritual plateau when he does not feel like he can just be himself and still be a Christian guy or man of God. Here again the average guy looks at his performance and believes the Christian life is one of performing good deeds and building on good thoughts and right living before God.

The average guy is still tied to the Man Code that says he must work for his salvation and for acceptance from God. He does not understand the transformation when a man comes to know Jesus, as Scripture tells us in 2 Corinthians 5:17 (NLT): "This means that anyone who belongs to Christ has become a new person. The old life is gone; a new life has begun!"

The new man can relax and still be himself. He will discover how the Holy Spirit is transforming him. That transforming process can be awkward at first, especially for guys who are still works-based in their theology. But it's a wonderful journey when old habits and thoughts pass away. It's like saying this man is "under new management."

Another way that a man will know that he has reached his spiritual plateau is when he believes other men have their act together. They pray, read the Bible, and act the right way at church, but he doesn't. This is a major false assumption of his, similar to believing God loves other guys but not him because he's much worse than other guys.

On the flip side, he needs to be reminded that **he's not the only guy struggling with specific temptations and sins.** Don't forget that the devil's lies and deception are to separate and isolate men. There are wolves out there in sheep's clothing that are after him. The truth is **other men do struggle and don't have their act together at all.** That's why the Bible encourages us to be in community because sharing our experiences can lead to breakthroughs. Even the smallest form of spiritual breakthrough is life-giving.

In addition, a man will know that he has reached his spiritual plateau when he tries to "manage" sin in his life.

What do we mean by this so-called "sin management"? It's a syndrome within Christian men who are steeped in works-based theology or certain religious beliefs for salvation, acceptance, and approval from God. **They believe if they are good enough and keep the rules more than they sin, then their good (or their works) will outweigh their bad (their sin) and they will get into heaven after they die.** It's the idea there is a Big Scorekeeper in the Sky keeping a running total of the good and bad we do in our lives. But that is a battle men cannot win because "no one is good—except God alone," Jesus said in Mark 10:18 (NIV).

Remember, sin manages men. Men cannot manage sin.

AN EXHAUSTIVE PROCESS

Here's a follow-up thought: doing good deeds, such as giving money to widows, orphans, and the homeless, is wonderful in God's sight. But how much do you have to give away to get to heaven? How much is enough? Just thinking—and worrying—about all this can be exhausting.

But that is what the devil does. He puts us under works and performance, whispering in our ears that we can never measure up or do enough. This is often why men walk away from their faith.

Let us remind you that God demonstrated His love for us in that while we were still sinners He died for us (Romans 5:8). He took care of it all.

If this idea about Jesus dying for you is new to you or this explanation does not make sense, **we encourage you to ask God for help—right now. Ask God to help you understand and apply Romans 5:8 in your life. Pray about it.** The time for breakthrough may well be yours right here and right now.

This is why the gospel or truth about Christ is good news. Your struggles to be a good person are over. Rather than playing the performance-based game of sin management, enjoy the sense of freedom and release that comes with a humble and trusting walk with Christ.

Rather than comparing yourself to others and coming away feeling spiritually inferior and like a loser, ditch the Man Code that says you must compete to get ahead in life.

Rather than comparing yourself to other men as a provider at home and on the job, be content with who you are in Christ and trust Him to provide for you and family.

A man of God finds his identity in Jesus Christ and makes Jesus his standard of comparison. This may sound like the toughest comparison ever, but Jesus is always giving grace.

His grace often leads to breakthroughs. Other men may reject or judge, but when a man comes into the grace room with Jesus, it's a powerful moment. Jesus sets men free from competing with each other. A newly free man can become an encourager of other men and fan their flames to grow as believers in Christ. This is a truth that sets men free.

We've seen how some men are afraid to get too close to anyone because they fear they might be found out for who they really are. This is another consequence of the fear of man and even the fear of self, rather than a fear of God. This is part of the devil's scheme to isolate men from healthy connection with other men because they fear judgment and lack of acceptance.

Simply put, men are terrified of losing control . . . really terrified. That fear, however, is rooted in man's total misunderstanding of who God is or believing that God is trying to catch him at life's most sinful moments, like a traffic cop hiding behind a billboard waiting to catch you speeding.

To the contrary, God is gracious and forgiving. Jesus said He "came that they may have life and have it abundantly" (John 10:10, ESV). If control-obsessed men understood God's true nature, they would not be fearful of surrendering total control.

Jesus said often during his three years of public ministry that he who wants to save or control his life will lose it. But he who gives up control for Jesus' sake will gain it (Matthew 16:25, NIV). It's a wonderful day when a man realizes he is not in control no matter how hard he tries.

"HE IS NO FOOL WHO GIVES WHAT HE CANNOT KEEP
TO GAIN THAT WHICH HE CANNOT LOSE."

—JIM ELLIOTT, martyred in 1956 as a missionary in South America

---

ARE YOU A MAN OF GOD?

We've met plenty of men who are either uncomfortable or puzzled by the term "man of God" and how it applies to him. Yet, they are curious about what it means to be a "man of God," even though they don't know how to become one.

Most men think a man of God has his act together and has reached some sort of spiritual pinnacle. He must have read his Bible enough, must have studied his workbook enough, must have served enough in the church, and must have a great marriage and children who are angels. **That is what the average man thinks the man of God is.**

If that were true, the list of real men of God would be very, very short. While we will expand on this notion later, let us make the observation that many men are uncomfortable stepping onto spiritual turf—meaning hanging around other Christians in a church setting.

The most basic reason we can come up with is that men generally avoid doing things they do poorly because they're insecure and unsure of themselves. Conversely, men don't like to be put into positions or situations where they aren't likely to do well. That's the way men are.

It's easier to work for personal success and people's approval than it is to pursue an intimate relationship with God. We get so busy seeking others approval that we forget that we already have God's approval.

This accounts for why men rarely share their faith in public or speak up to other men when they see obvious lying, stealing, and cheating.

The average man today feels uncomfortable standing on this type of spiritual turf because he probably doesn't like going to church. It's hard for a man who faces compromises daily at work and in the community to sit still and listen to God's truth or be confronted with his sin. He doesn't like facing up to his failures, although deep down he knows he needs to.

The man who has reached his spiritual plateau has a hard time identifying with the guy up there preaching in front of everybody. He likely harbors a misunderstanding about preachers, not realizing that they too are sinners and face daily challenges. When a preacher shows he is human or vulnerable, average men should be encouraged and able to identify with him as a spiritual leader.

As Pete says, "I'd rather see faith in action than hear a fancy sermon any day."

The average man could be afraid that if he really gets serious, God will make him go serve the poor in Africa and live in a mud hut. This is another fundamental misunderstanding of God's sovereign plan for each man. Oddly, when God changes a man, he is comfortable in his calling regardless of location. That includes being called to Africa or Australia, or serving orphans and the homeless close to home.

A man who has reached his spiritual plateau struggles with prayer. We can say that with confidence because men are often totally afraid to be alone in God's presence.

Why would God talk to me? the average man asks himself. *Why would I talk to Him when I have repeatedly let Him down?*

The point is **sin wrecks our relationship with God**, and the likely cause of that is unresolved sin. On the other hand, **God made it clear in 1 John 1:9 (NIV) that if we confess our sin, He is faithful and just and will forgive us.** Psalm 51:17 (NLT) adds that God "will not reject a broken and repentant heart."

So, confess to God. Remove self-imposed barriers. Take steps to God and open up in prayer.

Prayer is talking with God in a language both of you can understand. It does not have to be formal. Most effective prayers are informal. It's not about posture or place; prayer is about the heart connecting with God.

We encourage you to **start your morning with a prayer** (along with reading one Bible sentence or verse), and **close your night the same way** regardless of time, location, and prayer need. Seek God's face. Desire to know him. He already knows us in great detail. **There's nothing you can say that is a surprise to Him.**

A TIME FOR SPIRITUAL LEADERSHIP

There are a few more points to make regarding how a man knows when he has reached his spiritual plateau. For instance, if he cannot keep up with his wife spiritually and allows her to take the spiritual lead in their relationship, she may resent him for that.

As we said earlier, men avoid things they are not good at. If a wife is critical of a man's prayer life or spiritual leadership, he will pull back and stop. Wives get frustrated because they do not know what to do next. Just praying and waiting for God seems to take too long, so they try to help God "do something" about their spouse, but that rarely works.

A man who has reached his spiritual plateau fears sharing his faith because he does not know how or believes there is an exact "right way" to do it. Perhaps his greatest fear is spiritual rejection or appearing ignorant about God and what is in the Bible.

But you don't have to attend a seminary to share what you know about God and the Bible. Just be yourself, and you'll find that **down-to-earth guys really attract people to Christ.** Jesus wants us to be ourselves. Your humility will melt away and overcome fear. I (Phil) still clearly remember the first time Pete shared with me that Jesus prefers *availability* to *capability*.

We understand that in Bible studies that you may be asked to look up a Scripture verse and have no idea where to find that book of the Bible. It can be embarrassing to scramble through various parts of the Bible while everyone else goes straight to the Scripture.

Set that embarrassment aside. **It's okay to not start with fancy Bible knowledge.** Most guys can relate. We're all on a journey, and everyone in a Bible study should know that and see the bigger picture, which is, "All Scripture is God-breathed and is useful for teaching, rebuking, correcting and training in righteousness" (2 Timothy 3:16, NIV).

Another thing we see in the Church is that when opportunities come along to become a spiritual leader such as a deacon or an elder, many men believe they are not spiritually qualified to take on those roles.

So, he ducks and dodges and does a lot of fancy footwork to avoid discovery that he is not as spiritual as others perceive him to be or he knows he should be.

This is an accurate but poor reflection of men of all ages in church today. We do a poor job of preparing men to be spiritual leaders at home, work, and in the Church. **Men must learn and be trained with grace-filled modeling and mentoring**, but churches rarely minister to men. This means men in leadership are often not qualified or prepared to face spiritual battle and lead others.

So, if the call to serve in your church comes to you, will you step up? Or will you remain at the same spiritual plateau?

DISCUSSION STARTER QUESTIONS

> What is a false perception of a Christian guy?

> What is sin management? Can you do enough good things to outweigh the bad, and get into heaven? Please explain.

> If a friend found out who you really are, what would be your biggest fear? Pray to God about what you would say. Ask for His help. Humility, often unappreciated by culture, is embraced here.

> What are examples of grace-filled mentoring and modeling?

> Prayer is powerful, yet often misunderstood. How is it described late in this chapter? How are you most comfortable praying?

PETE'S PRAYER

Father, this spiritual plateau sounds a lot like me. Please forgive me for being focused on other things that often steal my joy, rather than focusing on You. Give me a love in my heart that I've never had but desperately want. Amen.

5
IDENTITY CONFUSION

For men, the times are-a changing, as the old Bob Dylan song said. Actually, the times have changed for men in many ways.

As fathers have been increasingly separated from families because of work demands and families have drifted from church over the past half-century, the factors that form the identity of a man have changed.

Once upon a time, fathers, uncles, and grandfathers shaped the positive stages of manhood. (And, unfortunately, the negative ones as well, we must add.) Church and community leaders reinforced the biblical and historically traditional roles.

That time has passed, however, for a variety of reasons, including the rise of what we call "extreme feminism."

We are not bashing women or trying to protect failed male standards, nor are we condoning behavior that treats women as inferior and not equal to men because we are all equal in the eyes of God. What we are referring to is an extreme feminist mindset that has emerged in the last generation. These days, men are not allowed to be masculine or muscular any more, which creates confusion in our culture.

Leo Burnett, a major Chicago advertising firm, conducted a global study of masculinity, which found that half of men say their role in society is unclear. Many men are not sure how they are supposed to act or what it means to be a leader in the family, especially a spiritual leader.

What we are seeing is a cultural quest to "change" men, and that quest starts in the nation's elementary schools, where **boys are routinely punished for being active, competitive, and restless.** As psychologist Michael Thompson, author of *Raising Cain: Protecting the Emotional*

Life of Boys, aptly observed, girls' behavior is the gold standard in the primary grades. Elementary school is not boy friendly. Added David French in the *National Review*, "As our society unlearns masculinity and feminizes every stage of male life, boys pay a steep price."

For sure, increased fatherlessness and the rise of single-parent moms have contributed to boys growing up without masculine role models. But even in intact, two-parent homes, the attacks on fatherhood in the media—in commercials, TV shows, movies, and Netflix series—are like a constant drumbeat. Clueless dads are often the brunt of jokes or shown as unreliable and low in character.

This is one major reason why it's more difficult than ever for boys to grow up and become men—godly men. We've heard plenty of single Christian women tell us, "It's hard to find a good Christian man," and we don't blame them. It's like **today's culture took away the male warrior's shield and handed him a pair of skinny jeans.** Too many young men aren't stepping up to become faithful husbands, good fathers, and honorable persons, but that's because they don't know how or what they're supposed to do. **Today's young men between the ages of eighteen and thirty-four spend more time playing video games each day than twelve- to seventeen-year-olds.** While women are graduating from college and jumping into the workforce, too many men aren't hustling to find work, aren't getting married, and aren't raising families.

When that happens, they become *marginalized*, as author and former U.S. Secretary of Education William Bennett noted in *The Book of Man.*

"We said, 'You go, girl' and they went," Bennett wrote. "We praise the rise of women but what will we do about what appears to be the very real decline of men? Increasingly, the messages to boys about what it means to be a man are confusing. **The founding virtues—industriousness, marriage, and religion—are still the basis for male empowerment and achievement.** It may be time to say to a number of our young men who are clearly past high school and college age,

'Get off the video games five hours a day, pull yourself together, get and keep a job, and get married.' **It's time to bring back men."**

Since many men fail to understand what their role should be in today's culture, they feel marginalized, emasculated, and that women are running everything.

CONFUSION ABOUT REAL MEN

One time, I (Pete) was invited to speak to a men's retreat for a large church that was filled with about two hundred young, vibrant, Christian men. I was excited when the pastors asked me to talk about "What Is a Man?"

But then I started thinking about why they asked me to speak on that topic. I figured the guys in that church were confused about what a real man is today. They could have too many options for what defines a man. Most likely, though, they have been influenced by a culture that has emasculated and marginalized them to the point that they were having little impact for Christ today.

Certainly, there are Christian men doing their best to serve Christ. They generously give money and involve themselves in their church or other ministries. But their numbers are far fewer than in the past. It just seems that we're not producing the kind of fervent male Christians needed to combat the onslaught of darkness that is engulfing our nation and the world we are living in.

I'm referring to a spiritual battle that has raged ever since Satan and his demons were thrown out of heaven. Satan's quest against God's power and sovereignty is the epitome of evil, wickedness, and sin. His war is against holiness, righteousness, and goodness.

In this spiritual battle, **one of Satan's strategies has been to discourage and neutralize God's designated leaders and warriors.** Actually, the enemy has been quite successful at this and all elements of society have suffered for it.

It's not that men have been in their best form throughout history, but in the last fifty years, **men in general and God's men specifically have been mostly absent from the front line at home and church.** It's like they refuse to grow up and take responsibility in relationships, the work they do, and their outreach to others.

They refuse to man up.

It's like the seed that falls among the thorns from the Parable of the Sower. All too quickly, the message of God's Word is crowded out by the worries of this life, the lure of wealth, and the desire for other things, as Mark 4:19 (NLT) points out.

"We believe," says Pastor Jack Hayford, "that if any civilization is going to thrive and prosper, it needs men who act like men when the need arises." **Jesus is our model when it comes to the roles that males should adopt**, roles such as:

- ⤢ standing in the face of danger
- ⤢ bearing up under suffering
- ⤢ sacrificing for the good of others

Boys and men have learned these roles, historically, from their fathers and mothers, but many of today's young men have been raised in single-parent homes by their mothers and with little or no involvement from their fathers. This means positive and traditional male qualities weren't "caught" by these young men while they grew up.

Satan, of course, loves this because he wants to take warriors off the battlefield or at least weaken their resolve, which makes them less effective when they become young men and start to have relationships and form families.

As our post-modern culture tramples on traditional and spiritual values, and as women have stepped forward in the home, in the workplace, and in the church, men have mistakenly stepped back. One of the innate qualities of men is being competitive, but given this evolving pressure to be not so competitive and more feminine, men look at leadership at home, work, and church as having everything to lose and nothing to gain. In their minds, when men compete against women, **they can never be right, helpful, or constructive by stepping up.**

THE ABDICATION OF ROLES

You see the fruit of this mindset regarding men in our education system. The fact of the matter is that fewer men are graduating college. In 1970, men earned 60 percent of all college degrees. In 1980, the figure fell to 50 percent; by 2006, it was 43 percent; and today male graduates account for only 40 percent of college degrees. This means men, as a whole, are being left behind in the workplace because a college degree is the entrance ticket to better and higher-paying jobs.

So instead of taking the initiative, men abdicate their masculine roles. Boy, do they! When that happens, women respond with resentment and criticism, and rightly so since these men are not pulling their weight. What's important to note is that men in the Church have no excuse for abdicating regardless of cultural influence.

From our time of working with men, we can confidently state that few understand manhood or what it takes to become a Man of God. They are not committed to reading the Bible, being in daily prayer, or worshiping the Lord the Jesus Christ either because they don't know how or have never seen that kind of behavior modeled. These men rarely have other godly men in their lives, and because of that, they are often unknowingly and painfully easy targets for the devil.

If men are to find their rightful place "for such a time as this" (Esther 4:14, NIV), it would also be helpful if they could get involved in an impactful men's ministry. Unfortunately, fewer and fewer men are choosing to do this.

CONFUSION REIGNS

Moving forward, and to re-state the premise of this chapter, men are confused about:

- ↗ what a real man is today
- ↗ their understanding of Jesus as a model of family, leadership, and courage
- ↗ what a "Man of God" is and how to become one
- ↗ what spiritual leadership in the home means or is all about
- ↗ how to become a spiritual leader
- ↗ what his role is as a Christian husband and father, and how to do it
- ↗ how to act as a Christian in the workplace or public market-place, and still be able to provide for himself and his family
- ↗ the value of integrity

In sum, men have been emasculated and marginalized. We have some ideas to help men overcome the impact of culture today regarding real manhood, and that starts with gaining an understanding of how God is calling you to be a man and realizing that Jesus is a model of family, leadership, and courage.

The old Man Code defined how the world looked at men, but the Bible portrays and defines manhood differently. **Jesus is the model—our example and the standard.**

At our Influencer West Men's Ministry meetings in Southern California, two of our favorite sayings are these: **"Men chase after men who chase after Christ"** and **"Any encounter with Jesus makes any man a better man."**

Jesus called men to follow him. His disciples were twelve average guys, but there was nothing casual about them. In Matthew 4:19 (NLT),

Jesus said He would give them a vocation, identity, and purpose. "Come, follow me, and I will show you how to fish for people!"

You too can become a fisher of men starting right where you stand today.

The world would say a real man must have his act together before seeking Jesus, but that puts an emphasis on what a man does today and tomorrow. Jesus puts the emphasis on who a man is at *this* moment.

In Psalm 1, a man of God is described as a man who does not walk with the wicked, sinners, and scoffers. This man does not hang out with people intent on harming him. Instead, a Man of God is called to meditate on God's Word day and night. The result is a good definition of a man, like **a tree planted by streams of water, which yields its fruit in season and whose leaf does not wither—whatever they do prospers"** (Psalm 1:3, NIV).

Prospering is not always financial gain. You can prosper when you are unselfish and helping others, especially when you are a mentor and role model. This is a very different man from the one who finds his identity in money, sex, and the idol of self.

The Man of God finds his identity in Jesus Christ. **He loves Jesus and proves it by reading the Bible, praying, and regularly attending a Bible-based church.** He honors his wife as a woman and the mother of his children. He raises children who know Jesus, leaning on Proverbs 22:6 (NASB), which says, "Train up a child in the way he should go, even when he is old he will not depart from it."

This is not that complicated. But living this type of life requires daily discipline, not of being perfect but following Jesus.

The rewards are not often outward or obvious, but they are found in the fruit of a man's life. His life is a transformation. **He is close to Jesus day and night.** He is willing and obedient one day at a time in the midst of life's joy and problems.

THE FRUIT OF THE SPIRIT

We stressed earlier that most of the things guys identify with in this life—wealth, power, and sex—are temporary and possibly dangerous when pursued in the extreme. Greed and lust are characteristics of those pursuing this lifestyle.

The opposite characteristics are found in Galatians 5:22-23 (NIV), which tells us, **"The fruit of the Spirit is love, joy, peace, forbearance, kindness, goodness, faithfulness, gentleness and self-control."**

These are the true characteristics or nature of our God.

This aforementioned list of characteristics should be a goal for every man, and they come from chasing after Jesus in faith and obedience. **These traits are life-giving, satisfying, and fulfilling.**

When a man understands and practices these traits, he no longer has to be confused about his identity.

Why is that?

Because now his identity is in Christ and His characteristics for right living: love, joy, peace, forbearance, kindness, goodness, faithfulness, gentleness and self-control.

Now that's a true Man of God.

DISCUSSION STARTER QUESTIONS

> Who or what molded your view of a dependable adult man with strong character and faith in God?

> What is the impact of marginalized men?

> Do you see evidence of men being absent from the front line of home and church?

> How do you take steps to learn about what a Man of God is and how to become one?

> How do you apply characteristics from the fruit of the Spirit?

PETE'S PRAYER

Father, thank you for the men You have given me in my life who have modeled for me both what a Man of God looks like and what a Man of God is not. I have a ways to go before I become the man You created me to be, so help me become one of those men!

6

FAILING AND SUCCEEDING AT THE IMPORTANT STUFF

The average Christian man sees himself as basically a good guy, though he doesn't help out or serve at church much. He tells himself that he's too busy at work and has too much stuff going on at home to pitch in when the church is looking for volunteers.

Truth be told, the jobs don't sound that interesting and don't match his interest, skills, or abilities.

Teaching children a Bible lesson in a Sunday school sounds like a fate worse than death. What if he stood in front of all those kids and demonstrated how little knowledge he has about Abraham and Noah? Didn't they build an ark together?

Volunteering to clean up after the church ice cream social also lacks appeal. And who wants to work a string trimmer and rake in the hot sun clearing out a bunch of weeds behind the church? Not the average guy.

And so he sits on his hands whenever the pastor issues a call for help from the pulpit. *Someone else will take care of it—or they can hire somebody.*

These days in the church, and in many cultures around the world, it's rare to find men volunteering their time in their local churches. The vacuum is filled by women, and it shows. **The generally held view of the Church today is that it's a destination for women and children but not so much for men.**

Pete says he's been asked many times why so few churches have a ministry to men. Here's what he had to say:

There are a number of answers. For instance, churches tend to shape and form around the values of leaders. Once, as a pastor of a church, our elders discussed our values and decided that we needed to focus on the 3Ms—men, missions, and marriage. The elders voted that way because those were my personal values and what I was focused on.

Unfortunately, most pastors have no great value for a ministry to men in their church. That is evidenced by 90 percent of churches not having a formal ministry to men. One reason they don't value a men's ministry is because they've never seen a healthy men's ministry in church. They also never had a Bible school professor or seminary teacher stress to them the importance of ministering to men. In other words, **they never heard they would never have a strong church unless they had strong men in it.**

If it's true men are threatened by relationships with other men, this also extends to leaders in the church. They establish ministries and decide how much time and money will be earmarked for those efforts.

I once sat in a meeting at a new mega-church. The campus included buildings for meetings and staff, a spacious chapel, and a parking structure on the sprawling acreage. There were all forms of ministry buildings for women, children, teens, and seniors.

"This is an awesome campus," I said. **"Where's the men's ministry building?"**

I received several blank looks, to which I said, **"Where are the fathers and husbands being taught to love their children and wives and be spiritual leaders in the home?"**

I knew I was asking a rhetorical question and there would be no answer, but I also knew they were good questions. If there was a fund-raising campaign for such a men's ministry building, I would suspect that women would give generously while men would limit their giving.

Finally, let me say that it's common for men to struggle living what they say they believe, which is why men will use that as an excuse not to get involved at church. When men say, "I don't go to church because it is full of hypocrites," I usually reply with a smile and say, "We have room for one more. Come on in."

NO WAR TO FIGHT

Author and speaker John Eldridge, who once said that every man longs for a battle to fight, an adventure to live, and a beauty to rescue, wrote that the Church is failing on all three levels.

"There is no war to fight," he declared. "No adventurous life. And there is no chivalry on display in rescuing women. Often women are confused and send mixed signals about wanting to be rescued but rebuffing efforts. That has not served women well for how God created them. Men are still called to the church, for sure. But not to dispel darkness with the light of Christ, but rather to attend regularly, serve faithfully and give generously."

THE ISSUE OF GIVING MONEY

Another leadership issue that we see missing in men is failing to tithe 10 percent of their income. Here's what God's Word says about tithing in Malachi 3:10-12 (NIV, with boldface added for emphasis):

*"Bring the whole tithe into the storehouse, that there may be food in my house. **Test me in this,**" says the LORD Almighty, **"and see if I will not throw open the floodgates of heaven** and pour out so much blessing that there will not be room enough to store it. I will prevent pests from devouring your crops, and the vines in your fields will not drop their fruit before it is ripe," says the LORD Almighty. "Then all the nations will call you blessed, for yours will be a delightful land," says the LORD Almighty.*

Most men do give something, but they lack total trust in Christ to actually give a significant amount of their income back to Him and see **the blessing from obeying God's Word.**

THESE TWO TESTS ARE TELLING

Pete always says there are two tests for men regarding Jesus as Lord of their lives: The first test is from the calendar: How does he spend his time?

The second test comes from his checkbook: How does he spend his money?

The reasons why men are in this financial pickle is because they have no budget, no spending plan, no savings, too much credit, too much overspending, and wanting too much too soon. It's like what Proverbs 18:13 (TLB) says: "What a shame—yes, how stupid!—to decide before knowing the facts!" Delayed gratification, once a common virtue and secret to success, is rarely practiced.

As the leader in the home, the first thing you need to do is gather the facts. You need to know how much you are paying for rent or your mortgage, what your car expenses are, and all the other household expenditures. Most people think they have a budget, but they really don't keep track of what comes in and goes out.

But the biggest problem is a lack of discipline with credit card use. That's generally why men and women overspend because it doesn't seem like you're spending money when your credits cards are swiped.

But you know, it doesn't matter how much income a family brings in. If you overspend with a household income of $40,000, you'll overspend with a household income of $80,000.

You see, people do not usually have a money problem. They have a lack of knowledge problem about money matters. They have not been taught guidelines for spending in the various budget categories based on their level of income. They also have attitude problems about money—problems with pride, greed, coveting, etc. This explains why the average family spends about 110 percent of their income living beyond their means.

By God's comparison, we are not wise, since Proverbs 21:20 (TLB) tell us, **"The wise man saves for the future, but the foolish man spends whatever he gets."** If we lived according to this proverb, we would eliminate 95 percent of all our money problems, but we're not listening to God. People don't understand that **the Bible is the best book on finances ever written.** Look at Proverbs 2:1-10 to learn how to make right decisions every time.

You can listen to God, or you can listen to the world. It's your choice. God's answer will allow you to provide better for your family, save for the future, pay your bills on time, eliminate worry and frustration, and honor Him with your tithe.

So how to get there?

Boiled down, there are only three things you can do:

1. Increase income.

2. Lower your outgo.

3. Control your future spending.

You need to make a list of ways to accomplish these things. You need to be creative and put on your thinking cap. Start by making a list of everything you will need to buy in the next month and stick to that list. Don't carry checks or credit cards. Carry only the cash needed for that day's planned spending. That helps eliminate impulse spending.

If you choose to be a good manager, God has good news for you: He will return a blessing greater than expected. "For God, who gives seed to the farmer to plant, and later on, good crops to harvest and eat, will give you more and more seed to plant and will make it grow so that you can give away more and more fruit from your harvest" (2 Corinthians 9:10, TLB).

What better thing than to bank on God's Word? The Book of Proverbs gives you plenty of practical instruction on the use of money, reminding you to advance the cause of righteousness with money but not to squander it (10:16); be careful about borrowing (22:7); and save for the future (21:20). The first ten verses of the second chapter of Proverbs remind you that those who listen to God's advice and obey His instructions will be given wisdom and good sense to make the right spending decisions every time.

Giving to the Lord's work, even as you're still working on getting your financial house in order, is all about faith and trusting in Him to provide and storing up treasure in heaven.

In 2 Corinthians 9:6 (NIV, with boldface for added emphasis), God's Word says this:

> *Remember this: Whoever sows sparingly will also reap sparingly, and whoever sows generously will also reap generously. Each of you should give what you have decided in your heart*

*to give, not reluctantly or under compulsion, for **God loves a cheerful giver.** And God is able to bless you abundantly, so that in all things at all times, having all that you need, you will abound in every good work. As it is written: "They have freely scattered their gifts to the poor; their righteousness endures forever."*

Please understand that **giving more or tithing will require doing with less**. That takes obedience. The call to sacrifice for the good of others won't be easy, but it's a call to keep churches from going into debt to pay salaries and mortgages. It's a call to keep missionaries on budget and fully funded. It's a call to **the rarest kind of faith—trusting God with your money and realizing it's not your money but His**. You are just stewards.

Finally, keep this overarching thought in mind: The greatest danger in life is not that a man will fail at something that is important, but rather he will succeed at something that does not matter.

DAILY READING OF HIS WORD

The average man rarely reads the Bible and is unaware of the personal benefit of regular early-morning Bible reading, prayer, and relationship with God. The average church-attending guy has never read the Bible all the way through. He may have started reading at the beginning in Genesis, perhaps a couple of times, but never finished. He has never been in a Bible study that has been impactful in his life. He could not find a certain book in the Bible if asked to look it up right away.

When Pete was a young Christian, he did not read his Bible much at first, but when he noticed a group of men quoting the Bible with authority, he wondered how that happened. They told him that they woke up early each morning to spend time reading God's Word. They felt like they were in the presence of God.

Pete knew that he didn't know the Bible, but he wanted to. "I instinctively recoiled at invitations to various Bible studies, although I knew I needed to be part of them," Pete said. "I knew if I wanted to be a man of the Word, **I had to hang out with men who were men of the Word.** I encourage you to choose your friends carefully. You will reflect them, and they will reflect you. You will follow them, and they will follow the direction of your life."

Jesus modeled for His disciples the discipline of rising early and walking away from the fire to spend time alone with his Father. You can look at this discipline as a matter of spiritual survival. Start with a reminder that you know who your enemies are—the world, the flesh, and the devil. Each are bigger and more powerful than you.

You need wisdom and strength, which are found in the Bible. Start your mornings with Bible reading and prayer. Begin your day in God's presence. We strongly encourage doing so because we know that men struggle with facing a God they believe is either disappointed in them or has openly rejected them. **But morning Bible and prayer time will help you adjust your view of who God is** and lead you to a healthy view of the grace and forgiveness God offers.

A CALL TO READ

Do you read books?

We're grateful that you're reading *Cracking the Man Code*, but in general, it's a question worth asking because it's our experience that many men *don't* read books, especially on worthwhile spiritual topics.

Women, who buy 80 percent of books purchased in Christian bookstores, often buy titles in the hope their husbands will read them, especially if the book has anything to do with their marriage and relationship. When husbands never get around to reading those books, wives make another deposit in a **resentment bank** toward their spouses.

What books will men read? Business books that will help them succeed in the marketplace or sports books about their athletic heroes. Unfortunately, many men will not get around to reading a book that helps them to grow spiritually, which leads to this point: **average men tend to have few spiritual goals.**

This is because the routine cares of the world choke their appetite for the Bible. Mark 4:19 (NIV) expresses this sentiment:

> *"But the worries of this life, the deceitfulness of wealth and the desires for other things come in and choke the word, making it unfruitful."*

That slice of Scripture applies today. The problem is what knowledge should you want or really need on a daily basis? When hungering and thirsting for righteousness is set aside because of daily cares, your heart is not hungry for God's righteousness.

George Barna and William Paul McKay, in their book, *Vital Signs*, wrote this:

> *Perhaps at no prior moment in history have so many Christians waged the battle for piety and holiness so lackadaisically and failed so consistently in their quest for righteousness. Pollster George Gallup said that never before in the history of the world has the gospel of Jesus Christ made such inroads while at the same time making so little difference in how people live.*

We urge you to heed Jesus' words, and **a good place to start is with the Sermon on the Mount.** The first beatitude, which is found in Matthew 5:3 (NIV), is "Blessed are the poor in spirit." This Scripture brings a man to the end of himself. A man must realize righteousness is nothing he can achieve, but he can receive it by grace through faith in Christ.

This leads to the second beatitude in which Jesus says, "Blessed are those who mourn" (Matthew 5:4, NIV). This is mourning over your sin that required Jesus to go to the Cross for your sins and die.

When you realize that Jesus called you to personal holiness as a personal disciple, you're ready for the third beatitude, which says, "Blessed are the meek" (Matthew 5:5, NIV). The transformation in spirit gives you a new humble nature that hungers and thirsts for God's righteousness and the fruit of the spirit.

This is the joy of the truth about God.

DEALING WITH GUILT AND SHAME

Are you struggling with feeling unappreciated? Do you want to be valued but basically you don't feel like you deserve it or, even worse, like you haven't earned it?

Men are often filled with guilt and shame. The devil uses guilt and shame to keep men out of the Word and God's presence. The remedy is to return to the first three beatitudes. The Sermon on the Mount confronts a man with his sin and offers a solution.

Here's the deal: When you realize your spiritual poverty, you discover that this is your entrance to the Kingdom of God. Knowing this should change everything for you. Knowing of your spiritual poverty should bring you to the kind of humility and brokenness that gladly leads to surrender, obedience, and freedom in Christ.

Since we're all spiritually impoverished, you need fellow travelers—family and friends that you can call on . . . especially friends.

We don't meet a lot of men who say they have "best friends," someone they can call in the middle of the night if there was a family emergency. In fact, we'd say that only 10 percent of men have close friends like that.

Too many men are afraid to be really known by other men. They don't want to risk rejection and disrespect if they are found out to be who they really are. They feel unworthy in the eyes of others, so it's better to keep relationships at an arm's length.

When you put your hope in Jesus, you can live for His approval—and receive understanding, grace, mercy, and compassion. When you live with this truth in your heart, you can feel free, and when you feel free, you can give yourself permission to have friends and be a friend. Living like you have nothing to hide is when deeper relationships are formed.

This is why being part of a men's ministry is so vital. Where else can a man find acceptance, love, and approval—from other men? Most likely not at work, where men (and women) are trying to get ahead and make the most of their expensive investments of time and money into their career. Sure, traditional service organizations like the Rotary Club or Lions Club or contemporary hang-outs such as a sports bar or fitness club are places where men can find approval, but a more surefire option is the men's ministry at your local church.

There's great value in a ministry that helps men discover the love of God, the grace of God, and the forgiveness of God through the acceptance and love of a group of men. That can open the door to the love, mercy, and forgiveness of Christ.

A WORD ON LEADERSHIP

There are four words that the average Christian man is allergic to: **humbleness, openness, transparency, and vulnerability**. The old Man Code does not serve him well in this instance. The leaders who have the ability and freedom to demonstrate these four characteristics would likely be men who have this kind of relationship with their fathers. These men are rare. Men cannot teach what they have not learned. **Men need leaders. They must be led.**

Sometimes we're like a herd of animals. We are reminded of the words of Isaiah 53:6 (NLT): "All of us, like sheep, have strayed away.

We have left God's paths to follow our own. Yet the LORD laid on him the sins of us all."

He knows all our flaws, but He found us valuable enough to send His Son to die on the Cross for us.

"I am the Gate," says John 10:10 (MSG). "Anyone who goes through me will be cared for—will freely go in and out, and find pasture. A thief is only there to steal and kill and destroy. I came so they can have real and eternal life, more and better life than they ever dreamed of."

Let Jesus be your gate to manhood.

DISCUSSION STARTER QUESTIONS

> What is the structure for ministering to men at your church? How can you get more guys involved?

> Where do you see evidence of fathers and husbands being taught to love their children and wives, and be spiritual leaders in the home?

> Where or how did you learn about tithing? **Do you really want to "test" God on this?**

> What do your calendar and checkbook reveal about you, your family and your faith in God? What did you read about wisdom for saving and spending in this chapter?

> Can you right now increase income, cut expenses, and control your future spending? Which is most easy and difficult?

PETE'S PRAYER

Father, I'm tired of missing the mark so consistently in so many important ways, but I thank you for Your grace that meets me at every turn. I want to be Your man doing the things You want me to do, and I know You will help me. Thank you, Father!

7

WHAT HE WANTS, BUT . . .

The average man in church wants good and spiritual things in his life, but only on his terms. Here are a few examples of what he wants, followed by the proverbial "bu-bu-but". . . .

- ↗ He wants to be a better husband and father and have a happily married wife and best friend, but not if it's going to take time being part of a men's group, attending couples classes, or Bible studies.

- ↗ He wants to attend church regularly, but he's reluctant to go every week because he thinks church is for women and kids.

- ↗ He says he wants to be in a small group with other guys and grow spiritually, but not as long as the study involves homework.

- ↗ He says he knows the importance of being part of an accountability group, but he wants to decide for himself what he'll be accountable for.

- ↗ He tells others that he'd like to do "spiritual things," like giving away food to poor families at Thanksgiving time, but he doesn't want to give up any weeknights or weekends to be part of that effort.

- ↗ He says he desires to be sexually pure and avoid porn, but he doesn't want to confess his sin when he gets caught up in its web.

- ↗ He says he likes the idea of being a servant to others, but he doesn't like being treated like one.

- ↗ He likes to make meaningful promises and commitments, but he always wants to keep his options open.

- ↗ He says he knows it's good to be humble, but he wants to pick and choose his spots.

- ↗ He understands that he feels better with a clear conscience, but he never gets around to repenting for his sins.

- ↗ He talks about being a man of character, but not if it means disciplining himself.

- ↗ He wants to be obedient to Christ, but not if it means giving up control.

- ↗ Finally, he desires to be in a leadership role, but not if that means attending a lot of meetings or going on retreats.

So how does the average man get what he wants *and* progress past the "but" or objection stage? Our experience with men tells us that personal growth and maturity are required, but neither arrive at the snap of a finger.

First of all, men generally have an aversion to reading, especially books that may challenge them like the Bible or books on marriage, raising children, and family life.

It's interesting to us that most guys *feel* like they can be better husbands and fathers but are clueless on how to make that happen. It's like saying you *feel* like you can become a better golfer but you never go the driving range to work on your swing.

Then there are the guys who go to the other extreme and believe they can never be good enough regardless of what they do. It's like the golfer who *does* practice his chipping and putting but is too afraid to play eighteen holes.

So we have a couple of questions for you:

- ↗ What price are you willing to pay to become a better husband and father?

- ↗ What are you doing right now to make sure that happens?

These basic questions apply to many things in a man's life, but it all starts with where you want to go and what you really want to become in life. How much are you willing to work on changing things or improving in areas where you're deficient or dropping the ball?

We're aware that men often fear the role of being a husband and father. Most married Christian men know they are supposed to be the leader in the home and devoted to their wives and children, but they get "stuck" in their ways. They aren't as motivated as they should be or do the things required to get better as a husband, father, and more spiritually disciplined man. **This is where a ministry to men can be very important—if not crucial—because other men can sharpen your game, as "iron sharpens iron."**

Men need to be around godly role models and mentors because it's impossible *not* to be influenced by those around you. That's why we tell men that they are known by the company they keep. If you want to be more of a godly man, then you have to spend time with other believers and mature followers of Jesus.

This happens by escorting your family to church on Sunday mornings and getting involved in a ministry to men. You want to be around men who will come along and walk beside you as they show you what it means to have a close, abiding relationship with Christ.

How does a man get motivated to read books and attend weekly meetings? More specifically, how does a man make spending time with God, as well as his wife and children, a priority?

The quick answer: by taking baby steps. Just as a thousand-mile journey begins with a single step, so does the journey to becoming a man of God. Don't think about what it will be like getting up at 6 a.m. every Thursday morning to attend the men's Bible study at your church. Instead, think about what it will take you to be there *next* Thursday. What do you have to change in your schedule? What adjustments do you have to make to be there?

This is not the time to be a "one and done" type of guy. If you attend a men's group meeting and feel welcomed, then make a commitment to be there the following week. If you understandably miss a week because of family or work, get back into the habit the following week.

Before you know it, you'll get into a rhythm of joining other men on Thursday mornings—or any other weekday morning—before work. Not only will you find other like-minded fellow travelers in this game of life who are no different than you, but you will gain friendships, form relationships, and be mentored by men who will disciple you.

Before you know it, you'll be *looking forward* to your next men's Bible study, and that's when personal growth from *giving and receiving* explodes.

FOCUSING ON CHRIST

There's something else you should know about joining a men's group: a Christian man does not focus on becoming a better husband or father to just improve himself. Instead, a believing man focuses on Jesus Christ to improve his *life*, which brings him into a closer relationship with the Lord.

"If my wife was married to Jesus, she would be married to the perfect husband," Pete says. "If Jesus was my children's father, they would have the perfect father. But I was never that perfect person, so I was never the perfect husband or father. My motivation for becoming a better father and husband found its energy in intimate, personal, vibrant, and even passionate time with a pursuit of Jesus Christ."

When you're filled with the spirit of God and controlled by His spirit, that impacts everything you are and everything you do. You will find time to read your Bible and grow to embrace that time. This is because your primary motivation is to become more like Christ. The basic general principle when it comes to a man's discretionary time is that a man does what he wants to do, values doing, and loves to do.

The apostle Paul put it this way in Philippians 3:10 (NIV): "I want to know Christ—yes, to know the power of his resurrection and participation in his sufferings . . ."

This is a powerful Scripture. A man whose heart longs after Christ, and has made becoming like Christ the priority of his life, doesn't have to be begged to read his Bible. **When he regularly reads God's Word, that man is on his way to being a better husband and father.** He may not have arrived, but he is on the journey.

When Jesus is your priority, He makes you a better husband and father because **He teaches you how to love, romance, and cherish your wife and give you principles for raising godly children.**

If you want a gracious and loving wife who is on your team and not on your back, then you must look for ways to love and help her by making her your greatest priority . . . after Christ, of course. In other words, she will never have a problem following you when she sees you obediently following Jesus Christ.

When you drop anything you're doing to give her your undivided attention, when you show her that you understand her, when you listen to her and take her seriously, then you will find an adoring wife who is more than willing to fit in with *your* plans.

When it comes to friendships with other guys, if you want a best friend—and most men in our experience don't have one—you have to first be a best friend. **The quality of friendship is often determined by your willingness to make others more important than yourself.**

In Paul's letter to the Philippians, the apostle writes that we should not look after our own personal interests but the interests of others. "Do nothing from selfish ambition or conceit, but in humility count others more significant than yourselves," Paul said in Philippians 2:3-4 (ESV).

So keep this thought in mind: when you gather together with other believers on a regular basis and are involved in a ministry to men, you're reminded regularly of who you are in Christ, why you're here on this Earth, why and how your family are so important, and where you're ultimately going.

The true test of a man's priorities, as Pete said, is discovered by looking at your calendar and your checkbook.

If knowing Jesus Christ and becoming like Him is a priority for you, then you will contribute to or lead a small group Bible study, read your Bible, do your homework, become accountable and responsible to other men, and sacrifice early morning, late night, or weekend time to be part of that group.

Let us say something about being accountable in a men's group. First of all, men have trouble with accountability groups. Somewhere along the line, they made peace with their decision that they cannot or will not discipline themselves, even though they know deep down that they will literally self-destruct if left alone. **They have a lifetime of experience living that way**, and the devil feeds on that.

Yet the main reason most men's accountability groups often fail is that **it's difficult for men to be transparent, vulnerable, and honest.** That is especially true about those things that cause shame and guilt. So if the group is asking you pertinent questions—which is what holding you accountable is all about—how should you respond?

With honesty.

With truth.

And humility.

SHINING A LIGHT

The beauty of the gospel is that Jesus Christ, during His death on the cross, called us out of darkness and hiding and into His light and freedom.

You do not have to protect, vindicate, or defend yourself before Him. **He knows your every thought, your every deed, and your every plan anyway.**

When you recognize the Light shined upon you, you will understand that you are a sinner. You cannot help yourself or fix yourself without Christ. It's who you are.

When you repent of your sins and confess that Jesus is Lord of your life, however, you will be humbled to the point where you know that you have nothing to hide. **That helps you be honest with yourself and with others, which is why a men's group opens the door to freedom.** When you have healthy relationships with Jesus Christ and others, including the most important people in your life such as your wife, your children, your extended family, and your friends, you're walking in obedience and discovering how to be the man, husband, father, and friend that God created you to be. Now that's what we call freedom—a freedom that can lead to a new level of faith, belief, character, and positive habits.

Now your heart is set on the Cross, not the crown. Don't think like the average man, who wants the freedom to sin without having to face the consequences, who wants to be glorified with Jesus but not crucified with Him, and who wants to be a known as a man of prayer but doesn't want to spend "alone time" with God.

We understand that men fail often in spiritual and everyday discipline, and simply have trouble adhering to rules. But you have two choices. You can choose pain and the consequences of sin in your life, or you can set your sights on Christ and the pain that comes from being reviled by the world for being a Christian.

We strongly believe that the underlying cause for lack of commitment to men's groups and Bible study groups is rooted in a man's aversion to continuous failure at spiritual disciplines. But this is not about failure but about pressing on to learn the truth about the gospel and how it works itself out in a man's life.

THROUGH A BETTER LENS

We're amazed at how many men view their spiritual lives through the works-based and performance-based mentality, instead of through the lens of a salvation of grace through faith. **Too many men mistakenly believe they have to earn their way to heaven,** a thought process deeply embedded in the average man's belief system.

As long as the devil can convince you that you have to work to be saved and that you'll be judged on a merit-based system, then you'll eventually run out of hope because you'll be sure that you can never catch up.

In addition, the pursuit of the stereotypical "American Dream" will eventually leave you devastated and confused because enough is never enough.

Maybe that's why atheism occasionally attracts attention. If God is supposed to rescue you from every pain and trial now that you've become a Christian, it's easy to conclude that He doesn't love you when life takes a bad bounce.

Some men may think either God is not powerful enough to rescue them or He just does not care. If that's how you feel, you missed the fundamental message about who God is and what life is all about—difficult, uncertain, and troubled.

John 16:33 (NIV) tell us, "In this world you will have trouble." Acts 14:22 (NIV) reminds us, "We must go through many hardships."

Contrary to the popular theme that you-only-go-around-once-in-life-so-go-for-the-gusto, **your life is not about yourself. There is something bigger than you happening out there.** As soon as you make peace with that thought, you'll understand that you're not in control of the future.

You're certainly not in control of when you will die (presuming that you don't take your life), but some day, you will die and your life here on Earth will be over.

The average Christian man has a real struggle with thinking of this world without him in it. He struggles daily with his own life and death. He tries to create heaven on earth but ends up building a misguided and self-centered world that ultimately never satisfies.

All of his answers, though, can be found at the Cross of Jesus Christ. That is where he finds his sin. That's where you will find yours as well.

Your sin—our sins—are what nailed Jesus to the Cross. His humility and brokenness kept Him there until He expired, but on the third day, He conquered death, which for us means that death is not to be feared because our souls will live in eternity with Him. **It's at the Cross where you find your model of giving up control.** He gave up His Son to redeem your sins and make you right with God the Father.

Once you make peace with this and realize you're a sinner in a sinful and fallen world and need Jesus, **you will find Him waiting for you with an outstretched hand.**

It's sad and a bit tragic that so many men today look for answers in therapy, new wives, different jobs, bigger homes, and in their own good works instead of finding all of their answers at the Cross.

This must be why Paul told the early Corinthian church elders in 1 Corinthians 2:2 (NIV), "For I resolved to know nothing while I was with you except Jesus Christ and him crucified."

DISCUSSION STARTER QUESTIONS

❯ What's one of the simplest things you can do to be better man?

❯ Do you recall the first time you heard about joining a group that ministers to men? Compare perception with reality.

> What do you say to invite a new guy to a men's group? Describe the process of taking small steps to spend time with God and eventually becoming a better husband and father.

> What does it mean to make others more important than yourself? How can a guy do that and lead a family or excel as a provider?

> What do you do when hardship far exceeds your ability to manage or control?

PETE'S PRAYER

Father, I am overwhelmed with Your goodness and gracious plan for my life. I know that I'd rather have the Crown without the cross in my flesh and not have to pay a price for the blessings You want to shower on me. I desire to know You and to embrace and fulfill Your plan for my life rather than my own. I ask you to bless me with the grace to attain what I just read in this chapter.

8

DESPERATE AND AMAZED BY GOD'S GRACE

One morning, I (Pete) was sitting in church listening to the announcements before the sermon. I was glad to hear the pastor mention the upcoming men's retreat because I was part of that team and looking forward to getting to know more men in the church. It's estimated that **only 10 percent of churches even try to minister to men**, and of those that do, probably 80 percent of those are struggling to do so.

"And now if you'll stand and say hello to the person next to you," the pastor said.

Ah, the dreaded meet-and-greet time.

I say "dreaded" because most men get uncomfortable real fast when they're asked to step out of their personal shell or bubble. I know that many guys feel awkward and uncomfortable just *being* in a church. Asking them to **connect and act friendly to strangers is one of the main reasons why a lot of men don't like going to church.**

I turned around to greet the couple behind us. I didn't recognize them, but that didn't matter. After saying hello to the Missus, I shook the hand of her husband. "Are you planning on going to the men's retreat?" I asked with a ready smile.

He squirmed a little. "No, just coming to church is enough for me. I don't need a men's group too."

I could tell this conversation made his wife real uncomfortable as well. She quickly jumped to his defense. "Yes, he's too busy with other things right now," she said.

"Well, that may be," I replied. Then I looked the man in the eye and said, **"You'll never be the man of God you could be or should be without other godly men in your life."**

I wanted to give him something to think about.

Our time was wrapping up. "Nice to meet you," I said as I turned around and sat down for the start of the sermon. As the pastor began explaining his topic that day, I imagined that the couple behind me was sharing the same thought: *Who was that man?*

Most likely, by his arm's-length response and her defense of him, I had just interacted with a wife who had been trying to get her husband to church for a long time. He may or may not have been a Christian. Perhaps she was hoping that I was the guy her husband would *not* meet because I might give him a reason to stop coming to church.

Years ago, I might not have been so bold, but I'd found over the years that God uses me to remind guys that **fellowship with other men can be literally life-saving.** As I've taught thousands of men over the years, **any encounter with Jesus Christ makes a man a better man.**

There is another truth at work here. **Men need other men in their lives for encouragement** as they walk through a landmine of relational, business, financial, and health issues. Too many men choose to go it alone, but that can lead to isolation, which is fertile ground for the devil.

The old sinful man's Man Code is rooted in pride, ego, and what theologian Oswald Chambers defined as "the insidious preoccupation with self." This Man Code keeps men in bondage and pain—or even worse. Some men get to a point where they feel there is no escape. For some, suicide seems to be their only escape from their isolation and pain.

Suicide? Doesn't that sound desperate?

Not at all. Men die by suicide three-and-a-half more times than women, according to statistics compiled by the American Foundation for Suicide Prevention. The suicide rate is highest for those in their middle-age years, white men in particular. White males accounted for

70 percent of suicides in 2015, and since 2009, the number of deaths from suicide has surpassed the number of deaths from car crashes. Each year, 44,193 Americans die by their own hand.

I can't imagine how desperate you must be to kill yourself, but it's a cold reality. The noun *desperation* is defined in *Merriam-Webster's Dictionary* as a loss of hope or a feeling of despair, a belief that the situation will never improve or change. This must be why American essayist Henry David Thoreau said 150 years ago that "the mass of men lead lives of quiet desperation."

A century-and-a-half later, too many men are still locked in the alcove of desperation, constantly living with anxiety and self-doubts. They worry about their futures and if their job or their retirement will be there next year, next month, or the next day. **They fear not measuring up to the world's standards**, their wife's expectations, and their children's innocent trust in them.

"CHRISTIANITY IS A RESCUE EFFORT FOR DESPERATE MEN."

—Walt Henrichsen, author of *Disciples Are Made, Not Born*

This mindset illustrates why many men believe that their relationship with God precariously hangs on their willingness and ability to keep the rules of "religion." They believe they should know enough, serve enough, give enough, work hard enough, and be good enough to merit God's love, acceptance, and forgiveness.

Like Isaiah, their constant attitude is like this Scripture: "It's all over! I am doomed, for I am a sinful man. I have filthy lips, and I live among a people with filthy lips" (Isaiah 6:5, NLT).

Men, in their roles as husbands and fathers, tend to feel that they do not deserve what they have not worked for. They feel unworthy of receiving gifts—especially the gift of salvation and even the gift of our heavenly Father's love and acceptance.

Even though the Bible tells us about God's love and grace, they feel guilty accepting what they have not earned. The average Christian guy thinks God is disappointed in him, and he acts accordingly.

If you feel you have trouble measuring up, let us remind you that God loves you and all of His children. He knows what you're up against and what lies in the heart of man because **He sent His only Son to live in human form**. God would like for men to do better and *not* sin, but **He is not surprised and does not love you any less when you *do* sin.**

Pete likes to say to men, "I don't know if you've tried perfection lately, but it's exhausting. People who are perfectionists take great pains in trying to get there—and then pass those pains along to everyone else. They rarely are comfortable with themselves or others.

"I believe the answer to us ever doing enough in our Christian lives is found and solved in the presence of God when we are invited to experience His grace, mercy, and accepting love," Pete continued. "When you can find peace with God in settling your sins, you will find that you can be at peace with all of your flaws and shortcomings. You can cut others some slack as well. What a concept! Peace with yourself, peace with others, and peace with God."

This is the abundant promise that Jesus committed to believers when He said, **"My purpose is to give them a rich and satisfying life"** (John 10:10b, NLT).

ACCEPTING GRACE AND FORGIVENESS

Men will not be fruitful for Christ or productive in their spiritual lives until they are at peace with God. Then they can bask in the freedom of His grace and love for them.

If a man cannot "get over himself," however, he will not be able to accept God's grace and forgiveness. Otherwise, all the work he does will be about him doing good rather than God's good working in and through him to others. This is serious business with the Lord:

> *"Not everyone who calls out to me, 'Lord! Lord!' will enter the Kingdom of Heaven. Only those who actually do the will of my Father in heaven will enter. On judgment day many will say to me, 'Lord! Lord! We prophesied in your name and cast out demons in your name and performed many miracles in your name.' But I will reply, 'I never knew you. Get away from me, you who break God's laws.'"*
>
> —MATTHEW 7:21-23 (NLT)

These verses highlight the difference between faith and fear, as stated earlier.

Fear comes riddled with guilt and shame for not doing enough. Fear carries the heavy loads of trepidation and unease regarding punishment and abandonment, which drives men to desperation and hopelessness.

The opposite of fear is faith, which focuses on Christ and His accomplishments rather than on ourselves and our accomplishments, or lack thereof. We can then experience freedom and joy, basking in the love of Christ and our Father God who has given us His peace and freedom.

Once you step out in faith, you can get on with the Great Commission as God designed you to be part of. You no longer have to concern yourself with doing enough because Jesus did enough on the Cross when He said, "It is finished."

Our Lord could have said, "I've done it! I've done enough!" In light of this, this changes the equation from (1) trying to do enough to (2) seeking to praise Him enough. They are two very different things. Let's explore that through one of Pete's stories:

It was a Monday night at church, and I was just finishing up a marriage class I was teaching when I noticed one of the guys from our men's group leaning on the doorpost in the back of the room. I had counseled him and his wife a few times and knew they were struggling. I'll call him Jeremy.

When most of the folks had left the room, Jeremy walked over and said, "When I got home from work today, there was a note from my wife waiting for me that said, 'I have moved out. If you have any hope of saving this marriage, go see Pete.'"

I was actually proud of Jeremy for being so quick to come to see me that evening; most guys would not have come to see me at all, especially the same day they received a note like that. But Jeremy came because he was desperate. He wanted to save his marriage. I knew his wife because she had accompanied Jeremy to our marriage class more than once.

Yeah, sure, it took his wife moving out to get Jeremy's attention and take action, but I have known many men who would not swallow their pride in such a stark situation. That is why this broken man came—to seek help. **Well, Jesus Christ came to rescue desperate men.**

It seems that only when we are really desperate with nowhere else to turn that most men will come to Jesus, who invited us to come to Him in Matthew 11.

Jeremy and I talked about his marriage for a while and covered ground that we have covered several times before, obviously to no real profit since his wife had left him. It had been a long day, and this horse was ready to head to the barn, so I decided to get down to what I believed was his real problem. I looked Jeremy in the eye and asked him this question: "Do you really want to be God's man?"

Jeremy looked away and thought about my question for a few seconds. Then he met my eyes and said thoughtfully, "Yeah, kinda. I listen to you in the men's group and couples class, and I ask myself if what you're saying about being a man of God is right. And my answer is yes. You're absolutely right. Then I think to myself, 'Am I going to do it?' And my answer is, 'Probably not.'"

We have way too many of these "kinda" and "probably not" men in the Church today, which makes us weak and impotent. We need men like the biblical sons of Issachar, the son of Jacob and Leah and founder of the Israelite tribe of Issachar, who understood the times and knew what Israel should do.

So, here's where I come down: Jeremy and the category of "kinda/probably not" men in our culture say they want to save their marriages but not enough to pay the price. The reason most guys answer "kinda" to the question, "Do you really want to be God's man?", is because an absolute positive answer would make them feel like hypocrites.

Even if they said a resounding "Absolutely!" as scores of men have said when they have been asked this question in our ministry, they know it's not true. Sure, they *want* it to be true and even intend it to be true. But they're stuck because they've tried so many times in the past to be a Man of God and failed so miserably over the long haul. They have zero confidence that they can become a Man of God or live their lives consistently enough to merit that title.

In other words, they have no real power or control over their own lives to turn into true men of God.

Yet despite man's fallen nature, there is hope, and that hope comes from only one source—Jesus Christ.

TRYING TO GET IT DONE

This story cuts to the fundamental reason why so many of God's men—who want to be warriors—are spiritually weak and marginalized.

They have tried it on their own and cannot get it done. They cannot get it done because they've been going to war in their own power, wisdom, and abilities.

"Not by might, nor by power, but by My Spirit, says the Lord Almighty," in Zachariah 4:6 (NIV). The apostle Paul put it this way in Galatians 2:20 (NASB):

> *I have been crucified with Christ; and it is no longer I who live, but Christ lives in me; and the life which I now live in the flesh I live by faith in the Son of God, who loved me and gave Himself up for me."*

And Jesus said in John 15:5b (NIV) that "apart from Me you can do nothing."

So, let us ask this question: **What part of "not by might," or "I have been crucified with Christ," or "for apart from Me you can do nothing" is unclear?**

And we have to ask these follow-up questions: **Why are so many men fruitless, unproductive, and discouraged about being a Man of God or having spiritual and moral authority? Why do we remain so weak?**

Many have never really heard the truth about Jesus. Or they may have heard it with their ears but not with their spiritual hearts. Some of those who hear the truth and understand it end up ultimately rejecting it, however. In spiritual terms, **they want to wear the crown but not go to the Cross to attain it.**

These men say that they believe God loves them, but that is more theology of the mind than a personal, intimate experience and knowledge of the heart. Their reasoning goes like this, and we know about this from personal experience because we've heard men say it: **"If I don't love myself because I'm such a loser, and others do not accept me because of my shortcomings, why would God be any different? He must not love me either."**

Contrary to this average Christian man reasoning, God does love him. Deeply! We learn in His Word, "God showed His great love for us by sending Christ to die for us while we were still sinners" (Romans 5:8, NLT).

For some men, this foundational truth may not be easy to understand, accept, or learn at all.

That said, most men really do not believe God loves them regardless of how many times they hear it. This unbelief is deeply rooted in his belief system and part of his worldly works-based way of thinking.

This is because no man can keep all the rules all the time. No man can ever achieve "enough." He will always fail attempting to do so because he is a sinner. We all are.

When he does stumble or fail, **it's inbred in a man to hate failing and losing**. Feeling like a loser can keep a man from following Jesus closely, let alone understanding the profound intimate love of a Heavenly Father. After all, why would a man want to come into God's presence if he thought God was displeased with him?

That thought is not new. It was Adam's problem in the Garden after he had sinned. His first response was to hide from God, with whom he had always had a great relationship. Adam had changed, and his great error was that he thought God had changed too.

Adam was now afraid of God, and he hid. He knew God said that if he ate from the forbidden tree he would die. Adam acted in a run-and-hide mode, not realizing that with God you can run but you cannot hide so you might as well come clean. **God already knows everything about you and everything you've done**, but that doesn't define who He is: a loving, forgiving God.

This is why most men have a fear of coming into God's presence in prayer, Bible reading, or fellowship with other believers. Having a wrong view of who God is can stunt your spiritual growth and may cause you to stray from your faith.

All men, in a way, are just like Adam. We sin, we feel guilty, and we hide from God, as if God does not know our sin or does not know where we are hiding. That is why Jesus left His throne in heaven to come rescue us in our hiding places.

Jesus did not come to this Earth to condemn or destroy us. We were already condemned. He came to save us from ourselves, our sin nature, and from slavery to our pride and ego.

KEEP SHORT ACCOUNTS

You might have a good understanding of Bible truths, but it's been our experience that no matter what men say about believing how much God loves them, the majority of guys have an almost impossible time believing that He truly loves them because of their consistent sinful ways.

If you commit to keeping short accounts with the Lord by confessing your sins as you do them, you get on the right track. Keep that in mind as you follow this next story.

On the night before He died, Jesus washed the feet of His disciples in an important part of the Last Supper. When it was Peter's turn, though, he resisted Jesus, which prompted this response:

> *Jesus replied to him, "Unless I wash you, you won't belong to me. Simon Peter exclaimed, "Then wash my hands and head as well, Lord, not just my feet! Jesus replied, "A person who has bathed all over does not need to wash, except for the feet, to be entirely clean."*
>
> —John 13-8-10a (NLT)

Pastor John MacArthur, writing in a Bible commentary, said, "It is important to get, really get, what Jesus is teaching here. **When we are saved or justified, the cleansing that Christ does is complete and never needs to be repeated—our redemption is complete at that point.**

"But all who have been cleansed by God's grace in justification need constant washing in the experiential sense as they battle sin in the flesh. Believers are justified and granted imputed righteousness but still need sanctification and personal righteousness."

Jesus has provided a way for us to keep our hearts and consciences clean before Him and others, which is to allow Him to wash our feet. **That means to cleanse and forgive our sins as we do them and confess them.**

Confession is important. John put it this way in 1 John 1:9 (NLT): **"But if we confess our sins to Him, He is faithful and just to forgive us our sins and cleanse us from all wickedness."**

We have seen many men bring God down to their level of human logic and understanding by consciously or unconsciously thinking of Him in terms of their fleshly tendencies, which are sinful and worldly. What a mistake! Thinking that God's love is not higher and more supernatural than your ability to love is foolish.

Somewhere along the line, a spiritually aspiring man must make peace with reality in his understanding of God, which is that he's not like Him! Hallelujah! Consider these verses:

"My thoughts are nothing like your thoughts," says the Lord. "And my ways are far beyond anything you could imagine. For just as the heavens are higher than the earth, so my ways are higher than your ways and my thoughts higher than your thoughts."

—Isaiah 55:8-9 (NLT)

Here's what Pete has to say:

> Simply, the Christian life is not hard . . . it's impossible! It's impossible for anyone but Jesus Christ. For me to try to be perfect as my Father in heaven is perfect is a futile effort on my part. I cannot do it. I tried. I failed.
>
> I did not understand that God gave me the Holy Spirit. The reason was that God might live His life in me and through me. Only Jesus can live the perfect Christian life. **His plan is to come into my heart and live His life in me and through me by the power of His Holy Spirit**. It is what Paul meant when he said in Colossians 1:27 (NIV), " . . . which is Christ in you, the hope of glory."
>
> We have already looked at Romans 5:8 (NLT) to try to understand these truths, which says, "But God showed his great love for us by sending Christ to die for us while we were still sinners."
>
> Before that, in verses six and seven, though, God's Word says, "When we were utterly helpless, with no way to escape, Christ came at just the right time and died for us sinners. Now, most people would not be willing to die for an upright person, though someone might perhaps be willing to die for a person who is especially good."
>
> Verses nine through eleven in Romans 5 are also just too great not to explore and meditate on:
>
> > *And since we have been made right in God's sight by the blood of Christ, he will certainly save us from God's condemnation. For since our friendship with God was restored by the death of his Son while we were still his enemies, we will certainly be saved through the life of his Son. So now we*

can rejoice in this wonderful new relationship with
God because our Lord Jesus Christ has made us
friends of God.

—ROMANS 5:9-11 (NLT)

In practical terms this means that **no matter how much you sin, God will not love you any less. And no matter how good you are, God will not love you anymore.** This is God's love that in the Greek is called *agape*, which can be defined as the "highest form of love."

A CLOSING THOUGHT

When you truly get that **God loves you abundantly no matter what, that's a pretty good day.** That means you have escaped the deceitful lies of the enemy of your soul. Instead, you enter the gates of abundant grace and experience unlimited love, abounding joy, and true life that will never end.

Are you rejoicing yet?

You should be because this is very good news.

DISCUSSION STARTER QUESTIONS

> Who are the godly men around you? Are they easy or difficult to spot?

> Do you have trouble measuring up? When did you realize God loves you the same when you sin or make a mistake?

> Was Jeremy desperate, or was he reacting to a desperate wife? What is the biggest challenge for "kinda" and "probably not" men?

> Why is it so hard for men to believe God loves them?

> Why are so many men discouraged about being a Man of God or having moral authority?

PETE'S PRAYER

God, I'm one of the guys who struggles feeling worthy in Your sight. I know it's wrong and that I am worthy in Your sight, but I'm so invested in this works-based mindset that I can't seem to shake it. Let this be the moment when You break down these walls of doubt and fear and set me free.

9

GOD'S GRACE, FULLY-AND SLOWLY-EXPLAINED

The way most men learn is through repetition.

The best way to learn and memorize Scripture is by reading a section or sentence out loud and repeating it over and over again. Keep the words and phrasing in your mind, close to your heart, and meditate on the passage, as it says in Psalm 1, "day and night."

This repetitive nature is what we are doing, to an extent, in this book. We are utilizing several of the same Scriptures to drive home the truth again and again, hoping that it'll sink in.

Your goal should be to take God's Word to another level by asking the Holy Spirit to enter and apply these Scriptures to your heart so that you can live in a way that He would want you to live. Doing so would be supernatural, life-changing, and transforming! When you're willing to accept God's unlimited, abundant, grace-filled love, you can make a supernatural, spirit-filled breakthrough.

By now, you've likely realized Pete is the teacher and I (Phil) am the student. Pete has about four decades of experience leading men spiritually, but he would howl if I portrayed him as a perfect man.

"The Counselor needs counseling," he laughs, and Pete is quick to admit that he has faults like the rest of us. But I'm clearly more of a work in progress as a Man of God, while Pete's spiritual maturity and decades of fruitful ministry are obvious to everyone who knows him.

As I come alongside Pete to talk about the topic of grace, I start by reminding myself to slow down to fully understand and apply God's grace to *my* life. I need grace just as much as the next person, but I'm challenged to comprehend what grace means again and again in the midst of daily pride and pitfalls. You may feel the same way, so take your time as you work your way through this chapter on grace.

THE DEFINITION OF GRACE

What is grace?

Grace is the unmerited favor of God, given to him who does not deserve it by One who does not have to give it.

Let this definition of sink into your heart.

When God extends grace to us, even though we are sinners by nature and do not deserve any measure of grace, it's helpful to remember that He does not have to give grace at any time.

God's grace is the antidote for sinful man. Grace covers and includes the full glory of forgiveness for every flawed man's shortcomings and sin, and we're talking about every man on this planet, including ourselves.

I (Pete) like to explain the concept of grace by saying that it's common to view God as a God who keeps score of all our failings and all of our sins.

We think this way even though Paul made it clear in 1 Corinthians 13:5 (NLT) when he explained that God's love does not demand its own way and "keeps no record of being wronged."

Let me share several other translations of this last part of this passage so you can better understand the true meaning of this point about God not keeping score of our sins:

"... does not take into account a wrong suffered" (NASB)

"... does not keep a record of wrongs" (Holman)

"... does not keep account of evil" (Phillips)

"... does not hold grudges and will hardly even notice when others do it wrong" (TLB)

Are you getting it yet?

God does not sit around all day with a scorebook tallying minor mistakes, life-altering wrong choices, and everyday willful disobedience. At the same time, this doesn't mean He looks the other way or that our sins are meaningless to Him.

He is not surprised or disappointed when we sin. He knows that if left to ourselves we are programmed by virtue of our sinful natures to sin. This is why He doesn't hold our sins against us.

God understands the big picture: we are in a constant fight with the world system that is always trying to squeeze us into its mold. The spiritual battlefield includes the devil, who is at war with us and does his best to get us to believe his lies. He moves about like a relentless, prowling lion who seeks to devour us through temptation when we are weak.

But the Bible reminds us that **"the Son of Man did not come to destroy men's lives, but to save them"** (Matthew 5:17, NASB).

And now, let me get personal.

One morning I was journaling and talking to God. Knowing that I cannot get anything past Him because He knows me perfectly, and realizing that coming clean before Him is the right and honest thing to do to keep my relationship with Him growing and healthy, I began confessing my sins to Him. I pointed out a particular sin that was a constant temptation to me.

I listened, and in my heart, I heard Him say that He was as tired of me constantly coming to Him about this particular sin as I was.

The next time I brought up this sin again, He shocked me by saying, "Is that what you want to talk about today?"

"Well, I thought we might need to go over it again," I replied.

"If this is all you have got, I'm out of here. I have other more important things that we need to talk about today."

Wow! I was shocked! What's more important to God than my everyday sins and shortcomings?

But we weren't done. He went on to say, "Have you confessed this sin to me before?"

"Yes, Sir, I have. Many times."

"Did you ask Me to forgive you?"

"Yes, Father, I did."

"Did I forgive you?"

"Yes, You did."

"Did you ask Me to help strengthen you so that you can defeat this sin and keep your conscience clean before Me?"

"Yes, I did."

"Do you believe I am going to do that?"

"I guess I did not, but I do now."

This is the day when I finally realized that Jesus took *my* sins—every single one of them—with Him to the Cross. He took my individual sins, including sins of the past, present, and future, plus my entire sin nature and forgave me of everything!

When He paid the price for my sins on the Cross, He finished the job there. He does not want me to keep beating myself up every time I sin. Sure, He wants me to be sensitive to my sins, quick to confess them and ask His forgiveness with a repentant heart, but He also wants me to believe that I'm forgiven and move on.

In other words, He has put all my transgressions behind Him. **He will never bring up my past sins again. That's a measure of His grace**.

The devil, however, keeps reminding me what a low-lifer I am. The accuser manipulates my guilty conscience to keep me beaten-down and feeling unworthy. I have discovered that God gets pretty tired of my self-loathing and shame-based thinking, as if I don't believe that Jesus' death on the Cross hasn't taken care of all that.

My faith in His death, my acceptance of His grace, and my brokenness before Him takes care of my daily sins. He wants me to turn to Him and rejoice in a Savior who loves me, forgives me, and restores me every time.

To teach me a lesson about this, God gave me a vision one day. The vision started with me walking into the gymnasium of the Boys & Girls Club where our church met on Sundays.

As I strode in, I saw that the bleachers were all rolled up and the gym was empty except for a small group of ten people gathered in a circle at center court. As I got closer, I noticed a guy on the floor in the middle of this circle, and the group was taking turns kicking him. I joined the circle and started kicking that person as well. Between shots to the kidneys, I turned to the guy next to me and asked, "Who are we kicking?"

The guy chuckled. "Take a look," he said.

As I peered closer, that person was me!

And then I heard God say to me in that moment that I will have many people kicking me around, blaming me, accusing me, and keeping score on me. Some are doing it with good reason, and some are not. That comes with the territory in a fallen world.

God then said, "I'm tired of you kicking yourself, tired of your self-loathing, and tired of you beating yourself up because of your sin. I have given you a path to stay clean and forgiven, and a way to maintain a clear conscience and a solid relationship between us."

What God wanted me to notice was that **He was not in the circle kicking me.** He never has done that, and He never will. Hallelujah!

In Romans 8:1, Paul made it clear that there is no condemnation in Christ Jesus, and **Jesus Himself said that He did not come to judge the world but to save it.**

The truth is, I am already judged by my sin nature and for the times when I act out on that nature. I have learned that this whole thing of battling my sins, the world, and the devil is God's way of keeping me on my knees and constantly trusting Him. God wants me running to Him as my refuge, my strength, and for the grace and love I need to keep me on track with Him and others.

This is how a man can stay current and in joyful fellowship with Jesus. Man, what a Savior you have! There is no God like your God. He is the God of love, grace, forgiveness, and hope.

He knows that you want to be His man and to honor Him and to glorify Him in all that you do. That is in the new heart that He gives you. He also knows that you are in a terrible battle with your old sinful flesh, aided by constant attacks from the world and the devil.

Here is the amazing thing. God hates sin so much that He gave His sinless Son to die on the cross in your place and forgive you of your sins when you repent of your sins and turn to Him for forgiveness. Then He gives you a new nature that hates sin and wants to be pure and clean before Him and for Him.

The apostle Paul explained in 2 Corinthians 5:17 (NASB), "Therefore if anyone is in Christ, he is a new creature; **the old things passed away; behold, new things have come."**

That means that the moment you were saved, redeemed, justified, and forgiven, you received a secure position in Christ. God accepts you, approves of you, and delights in you as you are. **He has forgiven you for all of your sins**. He believes you are valuable. He cares when you hurt, and He makes all of His decisions with your best interests in mind. He has secured your future with Him in heaven for eternity. You received His divine nature when He gave you His Holy Spirit, making you a new man.

You are no longer the same old average or casual church-going guy feeling guilty about sin. And you needn't hide or run from God because you feel unworthy or are unable to live out your Christian beliefs at times. You are a new creation! A man of God!

In this new life, you have been created at a new level of excellence.

Your old value system and the lies you believed about God are gone. Sure, evil and sin are still around, dogging your steps, but you can see them in an entirely new way now.

Sin and evil controlled you at one time, but not anymore. You are a new man living a new life every day. Now you live for eternity, not worldly things.

So get this, men! As much as we would like to hide our sinful deeds from Him and often deceive ourselves into thinking that we can, we cannot do it. It is impossible.

Psalm 139:1 (NIV) begins, "You have searched me, Lord, and you know me . . . **you are familiar with all my ways.**"

Be at peace with that, guys. It is more of the good news.

OUTWEIGHING THE BAD

There is another kind of human logic and thinking that makes sense to the unspiritual, worldly mind but has no basis or root in the Bible.

Here's the thinking: *When you die, God will haul out your life-long record of good and bad behavior and deeds. If the good outweighs the bad, then you get into heaven.*

Since Pete has been on a roll this chapter, he can't wait to knock this idea down. Here he is again:

> I often ask men this question. Perhaps you've heard it: "If you died today, where would you spend eternity?"
>
> Most church-going guys will answer, "Heaven!"
>
> Then I ask a question that is not biblical but gets to the point. "So, when you get to heaven and Jesus is at the gate and asks you, 'Why should I let you into My heaven?', what would you tell Him?"
>
> Most men give me a works- or merit-based answer to

that question, saying, "Well, I gave money to the church" or "I watched the four-year-olds in Sunday school."

You get the idea. But neither one is close to the correct answer.

Instead of all the good deeds you did during your life-time, you are saved by the truth Paul shared in Ephesians 2:8-9 (NASB), in which he wrote, "**For by grace you have been saved through faith; and that not of yourselves, it is the gift of God**; not as a result of works, so that no one may boast."

This Scripture makes it clear that what most of us men think is the way to heaven is woefully wrong and miles from the target.

The truth of this passage and the gospel are these facts according to the Bible:

- ↗ **You cannot save yourself** by your good works and efforts.

- ↗ **You can only be saved by grace**, which is God's unmerited favor.

- ↗ God does not have to give you this gift. **You do not deserve it and cannot earn it.**

- ↗ **Your salvation is a gift from God freely given, and you must freely receive it by faith and as a free gift.**

- ↗ Jesus' death on the Cross in your place is the object of your faith that must be received freely and humbly.

- ↗ There is no other way, no other gift, and no other way to the Father but through Jesus.

- ↗ Your salvation is purely and totally a sovereign work of God that you have no part in.

In other words, God:

↗ opens your spiritual eyes when you could not open them

↗ calls you out of darkness and into His marvelous light

↗ gives you the grace and faith to put your trust in Him and Him alone for your salvation and receive His unspeakable gift of Jesus Christ.

The only conclusion I can come to is that **salvation is wholly and totally a work of God** that is super-loving, super-gracious, and superbly done in His power. You cannot boast about anything that has to do with your salvation, or anything else for that matter, because you have not done enough good things to merit salvation.

Who would think of such a thing as God becoming a man through His only, much loved, and adored Son sent to die in your place?

Who else besides our incredible God could or would come up with such a plan of love, grace, mercy, forgiveness, and imparted righteousness?

Any plan you can come up with would likely involve you working to deserve your salvation and have something to brag about. Be glad you aren't in charge of this. I'm glad I'm not either. We would botch it up big time.

Praise God for His wisdom and His amazing plan that includes us.

ACCEPTING A GIFT

After teaching these concepts at a retreat one time, a man came up to Pete and said, "I don't like the idea that I can't do this myself."

Pete thanked him for his honesty, but he also knew this fellow was speaking for lots of men who cannot swallow their pride of needing to earn and deserve things they receive.

It's as if accepting a gift is unmanly. They believe that if guys cannot provide for themselves, then it's not healthy.

Once again, though, they've fallen for **the old Man Code thing, which is from the pit of hell**. The devil uses the Man Code to stock the fiery place of eternal torment with plenty of inhabitants.

This is how Pete discovered that the average guy in the average church does not understand the gospel and is in danger of not being truly saved.

Of course, it goes without saying that we're not the ultimate judge of who's saved and who isn't. But we feel obligated, as a pastor and lay person in the Church, to make sure that those whom God has entrusted to our care understand what the Bible teaches about how you can know for sure that you're going to spend eternity in heaven with Jesus after you die. Pete knows that he will be held accountable as one of God's spiritual stewards of His sheep. The Bible is authoritative about that.

One time, Pete heard the story about an ailing man who was visited by his pastor. This man must have been in bad shape because the pastor shared the gospel with the man. For the first time, this patient heard God's plan for salvation and eagerly accepted Jesus as his Lord and Savior.

When the patient rallied and got better, the first thing he did after he was released from the hospital was to make a beeline to the church that he and his family attended and seek out the pastor who shared the gospel with him.

This father of three children said to the pastor, "My family and I have been attending your church for several years. We have trusted you with our spiritual lives. If I had died, or if any of my family had suddenly passed away, we would have gone straight to hell. We were not saved. How come you never shared the gospel with us?"

Any pastor reading this should be sobered. Are you protecting the souls of those God has entrusted you with? Are you fulfilling the roles of pastor and shepherd? **Are you leading people to Jesus Christ?** Does your flock know positively, without a shadow of doubt, that they are saved and will spend eternity with their Savior in heaven when they die?

This is a reminder that you, as a husband and father, need to make sure that the way you live your life before your wife and children reflects the way you understand the gospel. In that way, they will want to know Christ because of the positive way you live your life and see that Jesus is the way, the truth, and the life and that believing in Him means they will have eternal life with Him in heaven.

DISCUSSION STARTER QUESTIONS

> What was your reaction to Phil's confession about absorbing and applying grace?

> What is grace? Why is the concept difficult to understand and apply?

> What's the simplest way for you to remember what Paul said in 1 Corinthians 13:5, that God "keeps no record of being wronged"?

> What is the big picture about sin? What's Jesus' role in all this? Why did He come here on earth?

> Confessing sin is good. How did God react to Pete's repeated confession of a sin?

> In Pete's vision, do you ever get the feeling that you are that guy getting kicked around?

> If you died today, where would you spend eternity?

> How can something so important be a free gift from God? Can you accept this gift, or do you feel that you have to do something to receive it?

PETE'S PRAYER

Father, Your grace is amazing. I can't begin to thank you for giving me the faith to believe and the grace to receive Jesus as my Lord and Savior. Lord, now allow me to be a man of grace and reflect it to everyone I know and meet.

10

BEING A MAN THAT GOD CAN DEPEND ON IN A CRISIS

The *Merriam-Webster Dictionary* gives us several ways to understand what crisis means, but the definition that stood out to us was this:

crisis: an emotionally significant event or radical change of status in a person's life

Many men today are in a crisis mode because of the unpredictable and corrupt world we live in, but they are also dealing with plenty of baggage in their lives: hurts, wounds, betrayals, neglects, persecutions, humiliations, unfriendliness, cliques, loneliness, guilt, shame, fear, insecurity, and the separation and sorrow of death. All these are all the inevitable fruit of a fallen world.

Mankind has been in a crisis mode ever since Adam and Eve disobeyed the one rule God gave them. That's when sin entered the heart of man and altered us beyond repair by anyone except for God, who created us in the first place. If you can make peace with crisis in your life, it's our contention that you'll better cope with a crumbling world.

FINDING PEACE

Jesus said in John 16:33 that in this world we would have trials and tribulation, but we can take heart because He has overcome the world. Trials cause trouble in our lives, and Job 5:7 reminds us that people are born for trouble as readily as sparks fly upward. The only place to find peace is in Him!

But you can expect trouble. We tell our men that if they stay on the field long enough, they're going to face attacks, catch spears thrown in their direction, and be wounded. In other words, they will come face-to-face with trials and tribulations.

When you look at the present events and past history of mankind going its own way without acknowledging God, it's not a stretch to conclude that sinful man—when left to his own devices—will self-destruct sooner or later. Perhaps we're seeing that unfolding in today's hyper-partisan political climate, where the Judeo-Christian moorings of our country, based on the belief that all men are created equal and endowed by our Creator with certain unalienable rights—life, liberty, and the pursuit of happiness—are being shaken to the foundation.

A THOUGHT FROM PHIL

This is not about politics to the right, left, or center. Jesus followed up "Love your neighbor as yourself' with "Love your neighbor as I have loved you," which means sacrifice yourself for your neighbor. Jesus said in Matthew and Luke to make enemies your friends and expect nothing in return.

This type of thinking is clearly contrary to today's culture, but maybe it shouldn't be.

Those foundational truths and beliefs, also echoed by President Abraham Lincoln in the Gettysburg Address, are rooted in the biblical principle of valuing and respecting others whoever they might be, and **thinking of others as more important than yourself.** We consider this nation's Founding Fathers to be people of character and worthy of respect, but like every man, they were far from perfect. Despite their flaws, they formed perhaps the most remarkable nation and culture the world has ever seen.

As is the nature of things in a fallen world, there is a rise to nations, and there is a fall. There can be no denying that our country has largely turned its back on God in the last fifty years, and we are reaping what we have sown. This is seen in the disintegration of the two-parent, intact family. Four out of every ten children are born out of wedlock in the United States, but even more disconcerting is that the figure is considerably higher in the Latino and African-American communities, where 53 percent and 71 percent of children are born out of wedlock, respectively.

This development portends all sorts of societal troubles. We've seen firsthand how young men who grew up without a father in the home have great difficulty relating to God as a father figure. We should take great pains to love these young, fatherless men and show them in the Bible where God is described as a "father to the fatherless" in Psalm 68:5 and how Jesus said, in John 16:27 (NLT), "For the Father himself loves you dearly."

Keep in mind that of all the ways that God Almighty could choose to relate to humanity, He spoke the language of the family. Instead of referring to Himself as a benevolent king or kind overlord, **He chose the word** *father*, **which denotes strength, protection, and provision.**

Even if you never knew your earthly father or grew up with a father who treated you poorly, as was Phil's case, you will always have God the Father who loves, cherishes, protects, and values you.

God has a special place in His heart for the fatherless. **Psalm 27:10 says that even if your father (or mother) has abandoned you, He will hold you close.** You can give all your worries and cares to God, for He cares about you, says 1 Peter 5:7.

There's no doubt life is doubly hard without a father in your life. Jesus tells us that we can come to Him and learn from Him because He's gentle and humble of heart. We can find rest for our souls because He invites us to share the yoke with Him, for His yoke is easy and His burden is light (Matthew 11:28-30).

Let Him be the father you never had. Draw close to Him, and He will wrap an arm around your shoulder and lead you on a path that will lead you to a fuller, richer, and more content life than you could ever imagine.

BECOME BOLD AS A LION

Another insight into the meaning of crisis is that it's an unstable or crucial time or state of affairs in which a decisive change is impending.

These days we often hear of the impending doom of our financial system, how the dollar will collapse and lose its value, how inflation will run rampant, and how the sand pile of our national debt beneath us will erode completely, leading to a catastrophic breakdown of our financial system. We hear how biblical, traditional marriage and the nuclear family is disintegrating as we watch the next generation become addicted to opioids, meth, pot, casual sex, binge drinking, and video games. There seems to be very little that we can do about these various crisis points.

In the face of these ominous signs, **God has not given us a spirit of timidity. He has given us power to be as He is—as bold as lions and as gentle as doves.** God expects you to have such confidence in Him that He can count on you in the midst of today's crises and stave off the deceiver through the power of His Holy Spirit, as your holy, loving Jesus did when He went into the desert for forty days to fast and pray.

Only men who know they're unable to do anything apart from Christ will be the dependable ones in a time of crisis. They will be dependable because they depend on Christ and His power and strength. Be that person that the Lord can depend on in a time of crisis.

How can you be sure that you're dependent on Christ?

These verses from the Good News Translation of Psalm 62:5-12 nail it:

I depend on God alone;
I put my hope in him.
He alone protects and saves me; he is my defender,

and I shall never be defeated.

My salvation and honor depend on God; he is my strong
protector; he is my shelter.

Trust in God at all times, my people. Tell him all your
troubles, for he is our refuge.

Human beings are all like a puff of breath; great and small
alike are worthless. Put them on the scales, and they
weigh nothing; they are lighter than a mere breath.
Don't put your trust in violence; don't hope to gain any-
thing by robbery; even if your riches increase, don't de-
pend on them.

More than once I have heard God say that power belongs
to him and that his love is constant. You yourself, O Lord,
reward everyone according to their deeds.

God understands the average and flawed man. And in His grace, God still chooses average and flawed men to be spiritual leaders and followers. In other words, He still chooses any one of us because we're *all* average and flawed. No one is good except for God alone (Mark 17:18), which means that since we don't measure up, knowing where we stand in the pecking order should make it easy for us to depend on Him.

What God is looking for from you is total abandonment and absolute trust in Him. **Even if you're been a casual Christian or living a life of quiet desperation, God wants to use you,** as this Scripture details:

Remember, dear brothers and sisters, that few of you were
wise in the world's eyes or powerful or wealthy when God
called you. Instead, God chose things the world considers
foolish in order to shame those who think they are wise. And
he chose things that are powerless to shame those who are

powerful. God chose things despised by the world, things counted as nothing at all, and used them to bring to nothing what the world considers important. As a result, no one can ever boast in the presence of God.

God has united you with Christ Jesus. For our benefit God made him to be wisdom itself. Christ made us right with God; he made us pure and holy, and he freed us from sin.

—1 CORINTHIANS 1:26-30 (NLT)

God's heart was full of grace when Jesus chose the original twelve disciples. Our Lord had to see something special in men who lacked education, wisdom, and social standing—characteristics they could not see in themselves.

Trust Him that He's calling you to be His disciple and impact others—through your life, through your relationships, and through your words.

DISCUSSION STARTER QUESTIONS

> There's no way the world is in crisis, right? Life doesn't really have to be hard, does it? How have those statements worked in your life?

> What's an indication that God speaks the language of a family?

> Do you want to be a man God depends on in a crisis?

> What are the characteristics of a man who recognizes God in a crisis?

> When times turn tough, what kind of spirit has God given you?

❯ As you read deeper into this book, do you feel that God is calling you to come closer to Him?

PETE'S PRAYER

Lord Jesus, You've made it clear that men are part of Your chosen plan to be the dependable and faithful to the gospel. Thank you for calling me to this sacred responsibility. May I make You look good to the world in the opportunities You give me to put my confidence in You and You alone.

11
WHEN EVEN MORE GRACE IS NEEDED

I (Pete) grew up in a church that was fire and brimstone, all the time. Our preacher from the Deep South worked himself into a pretty good sweat with an oratorical depiction of hell as a place you didn't want to go after you breathed your last. His fiery description of hell as an unpleasant address for unrepentant sinners was enough to get me to turn from the error of my ways.

You don't witness "hellfire preaching" much these days, but back then, dynamic pastors let those in the church pews have it with both barrels, saying that hell was real and those who sin and do not seek God's mercy were destined to burn for eternity. They put the fear of God in you by quoting Scriptures such as these:

> *"Then the King will turn to those on the left and say, 'Away with you, you cursed ones, into the eternal fire prepared for the devil and his demons."*
>
> MATTHEW 25:41, NLT

> *"He is ready to separate the chaff from the wheat with his winnowing fork. Then he will clean up the threshing area, gathering the wheat into his barn but burning the chaff with never-ending fire."*
>
> MATTHEW 3:12, NLT

I had no problem understanding that I was a sinner. I got the message loud and clear that I was going straight to hell if I did not stop sinning and get right with God. And I wanted to be on the right side of heaven.

So, I did what they told me to do. I went forward. I accepted Jesus into my heart. I got baptized. I told my friends I was a Christian.

I discovered fairly quickly, however, that I didn't stop sinning. Not only that, but stopping all my sinning was going to be a problem.

To be clear, **I knew I proved that I was a sinner every day**. As David wrote in Psalm 51:3 (NLT), "For I recognize my rebellion; it haunts me day and night." My problem was that I didn't know what I could do to stop sinning or deal with my guilt and shame.

The apostle Paul had a similar dilemma and described it in the Book of Romans in this way:

> The trouble is with me, for I am all too human, a slave to sin. I don't really understand myself, for **I want to do what is right, but I don't do it. Instead, I do what I hate.** But if I know that what I am doing is wrong, this shows that I agree that the law is good. So I am not the one doing wrong; it is sin living in me that does it.
>
> And I know that nothing good lives in me, that is, in my sinful nature. **I want to do what is right, but I can't. I want to do what is good, but I don't. I don't want to do what is wrong, but I do it anyway.** But if I do what I don't want to do, I am not really the one doing wrong; it is sin living in me that does it. I have discovered this principle of life—that when I want to do what is right, I inevitably do what is wrong. I love God's law with all my heart.
>
> But there is another power within me that is at war with my mind. This power makes me a slave to the sin that is still within me. Oh, what a miserable person I am! Who will free

me from this life that is dominated by sin and death? Thank
God! The answer is in Jesus Christ our Lord. So you see how
it is: In my mind I really want to obey God's law, but because
of my sinful nature I am a slave to sin.

So now there is no condemnation for those who belong to
Christ Jesus. And because you belong to him, the power of
the life-giving Spirit has freed you from the power of sin that
leads to death.

—Romans 7:14b-25, 8:1-2 (NLT)
with boldface added for emphasis

But here's another verse that Paul wrote that put everything in perspective for me:

God saved you by His grace when you believed. *And you*
can't take credit for this; it is a gift from God. Salvation is not
a reward for the good things we have done, so none of us
can boast about it.

—Ephesians 2:8-9 (NLT)
with boldface added for emphasis

Like most guys, I had never gotten the grace part of this spiritual life thing. What a huge miss—like a placekicker shanking an extra point as time expires to lose the biggest game of the year!

Grace, which is defined as unmerited favor given to one who does not deserve it by the One who did not have to give it, is the antidote for sinners like you and me.

I love this definition. I love grace!

What a deal God has given you. We're all big sinners, wracked with guilt and shame, but you can be forgiven for all of your sins because God, unlike any other god, is a God of unmerited favor. He is the God of the immeasurable enjoyment of His favor.

He is the God who promises to put your sins behind Him "as far as the east is from the west," it says in Psalm 103:12 (NIV). **He keeps no record of your sins**, and He looks at you and sees the righteousness of Christ instead of your sin and shortcomings.

When you come to Him, there is no condemnation. He is gentle and humble of heart, and He gives rest to your beaten-down, weary, and heavy-laden soul. How about that!

Don't be trapped on the treadmill of spiritual performance and sin management. Instead, become the recipient of God's grace and mercy.

YOU CAN BE AT PEACE

The principle of grace is not a slam-dunk for some people, however. Consider this insight from Fil Anderson, a Fuller Seminary graduate and former Young Life National Director of Training. Writing in his book, *Running on Empty*, Anderson noted that he had been a struggling Christian for thirteen years because of turmoil in his heart. **"My problem is that I am never at peace and am always trying to be good or better. I am so afraid of making mistakes,"** he said.

That is what a works-based trap does for well-meaning believers in Christ. They tend to think how nice they have to be or how much good they have to do to gain God's forgiveness and acceptance. They just can't erase the thinking that they can never do enough.

Anderson now realizes that he was caught in a performance-trap lie, which presented him with all kinds of unrealistic expectations. "I attempted impossible performances to try to get God's approval by keeping a lot of legalistic or strict rules," he wrote in *Running on Empty*. "I thought I had to earn His love, and that caused me to almost take my life."

And then Anderson wrote this:

I want to be used more effectively for the Lord, but I feel so unworthy. I am such a failure I cannot stand to live with myself. I had such a wonderful conversion and in many ways am a "new creature in Christ," but I can be characterized by two words: anger and resentment. It is almost like I go through a hate cycle against the people I love the most. Afterwards I am so sorry and get very depressed. I guess I am angriest because I am not having spiritual victory.

That's the kind of desperation the devil is after. He wants you to think you cannot be good enough for God no matter how hard you try.

I love explaining to people that grace is the antidote for those caught in the performance trap and sin management like Fil Anderson was gripped by.

When I hear stories like Fil's, I wonder: *What is his church teaching?* Because too many well-meaning believers are miserable and getting bludgeoned by the enemy. They do not know what to do with their sin other than try hard, harder again, and even harder to be good.

Men, please read carefully. We've been taught about our disease, which is sin. **But somehow, we've missed the part about the antidote, which is grace.**

Maybe the problem is that we're not being taught about how we are in a daily spiritual battle with the world, our flesh, and the devil. Because of the spiritual warfare happening around us, we can't stand up to the onslaught 100 percent of the time because we are imperfect beings with sinful natures.

But if men hear that God desperately desires to reconcile us to Himself, to heal our spiritual hearts and bodies, and to bless us while extending grace when we fall short of the mark and sin, then we can go through life with an amazed look on our faces because grace, in these circumstances, is simply amazing.

Remember, a male characteristic is to stop doing things he's no good at. If you stink at taking care of the car or the front lawn, you'll quit trying. If your wife tells you that you're a lousy husband, you'll make a prophet out of her.

It follows that if you're no good at being a Christian because of a performance-based approach, you'll quit trying to raise your spiritual game. In fact, you'll mail it in, settling for being average and casual in the church—not too much effort but not too little.

That's why too many guys, when asked to be in a Bible study or lead a missions effort, find a good excuse to demur.

That's what casual guys are good at.

YOU CAN'T EARN SALVATION

The doctrine of God's undeserved grace has always been in danger of subtle changes from the original meaning. Many find that exalting works at the expense of grace to be a hard concept to resist.

The concept of working to earn salvation is deeply rooted in the average Christian's life and thinking. One of the sad aspects of this pride-based approach is that people want to earn their salvation, rather than receive it.

I ask you to latch on to this teaching of grace like a person thrown overboard reaching for a life preserver. Your spiritual understanding about God must start with focusing on what He gives you, rather than what you do for Him. You need to understand that **no matter how much good you do, God cannot love you any more than He already does.**

At the same time, **no matter how much evil you sink into, He will not love you any less.**

By now, we hope that we've built the case that this is what grace and unconditional love is all about, guys. What a God!

Yes, you have a glorious God that you may call upon any time you want. You can tap into His power to live the life He has given you at the highest level. His amazing grace makes it possible for you to be forgiven and become a Man of God, not based on your goodness, but on His.

His grace comes with a guarantee that God:

- ⬈ is true, lasting, solid, sure, and cannot be changed or shaken
- ⬈ can be known and not just hoped for
- ⬈ will never change
- ⬈ will protect you and keep you from spiritual harm

I have a framed quote that has hung on my living room wall for years, which some say is a paraphrase of Romans 8:28:

> *The Lord may not have planned*
> *that this should overtake me,*
> *but He has most certainly permitted it.*
>
> *Therefore, though it were an attack*
> *of an enemy, by the time it reaches me,*
>
> *It has the Lord's permission and therefore all is well.*
>
> *He will make it work together*
>
> *With all life's experiences for good.*
>
> —Anonymous

This framed quote reminds me that any troubles and trials that come my way will be used by God for His good. God's loving sovereignty reigns over my life and yours as well. This absolute truth can steady you when you're panicking, strengthen your faith when you're wavering, and give you peace when fear has its ugly hands around your throat. It has steadied me and Phil while we have faced some of life's biggest challenges during the writing of this book.

The Lord will make it work together until you go home to that final place of peace in His presence. And that will happen in His perfect timing.

I would like to end this chapter by sharing my thoughts in a devotional way:

God's Timing

When I'm hungry,
He's my bread.

When I'm thirsty,
He satisfies my thirst.

When I'm threatened,
He's my refuge.

When I'm shaky,
He's my Rock.

When I'm down and am ready to give up,
He gives me hope.

When I can't find my way,
He opens a door.

When I need wisdom,
I need only to ask Him without doubting.

When I feel alone,
He is always with me and
will never leave me.

When I'm weak,
He's my strength.

When I am inadequate,
I find my adequacy in Him.

When I don't know,
He comforts me by reminding me
that He knows everything.

When I'm afraid,
He will comfort me.

When it's not working and
all seems to be falling apart,
in Him all things hold together
(Colossians 1:17, NIV).

When I don't feel that He is there,
it doesn't mean He's not.

When my faith is weak,
He'll take however much I have
and move mountains for me.

When I'm blowing it big time,
He will be patient with me.

When I come beaten down and exhausted,
I can always crawl up in His arms.

When I'm too big for my britches,
He will humble me.

When I need to be rebuked,
He will rebuke me.

When I need training in
righteousness or His character,
He is faithful to me.

When all have forsaken me,
He is still there for me.

When no one believes me,
He still believes.

When I doubt myself,
He says that's okay but just
make sure I don't doubt Him.

When I hate myself,
He still loves me.

When I feel guilty,
He understands.

When I obey,
He blesses me.

When I sin and confess it to Him,
He is quick to forgive and restore me.

When I disobey,
He disciplines me as a loving
Father would and should.

When I run away,
He waits daily for my return.

When I'm sick,
He heals me.

When I die,
He will have His angels usher me
into His glorious presence.

DISCUSSION STARTER QUESTIONS

❯ Was there a time when you thought God gave you grace? What was that like?

❯ Do you really think God would make it so hard to live a life that pleases Him?

❯ How do you feel about knowing that you don't have to work so hard to get God's approval?

PETE'S PRAYER

Thank You Lord for the sure promise of Your presence, love, grace, protection and provision. Thank you for being the rock beneath my feet and the shelter from the storms of my life. May I tarry in Your presence and soak in Your blessings that I might walk on the raging waters of the trials and pain that are sure to come my way, as I keep my eyes on You.

12

ON BECOMING A MAN OF GOD

One Saturday morning at a men's retreat held at a Southern California church, I (Pete) was looking forward to teaching an attentive group of young men about what a Man of God was and what he was not. It's been my experience that most men have a misunderstanding of what a Man of God is, certainly according to what the Lord has shown me.

The average Christian guy is sure that a Man of God has his act together at home, work, church, and in the community. Guys think: *a Man of God must be an awesome dude!*

After making this point in my talk, I asked my audience, "If this is the definition or profile of a Man of God—someone who has it all together? If so, how many men do you know who fit that mold?"

I didn't hear any affirmative responses or see any raised hands in my audience. That didn't surprise me. Most men cannot think of *one* person who fits that mold of a Man of God. And if they can, it's probably no more than one or two guys.

"Do you really think God would make it that hard for men who love Him to be a Man of God?" I asked.

I saw some bewildered looks. I could tell that some of the guys were thinking.

"What if there was another definition? What if a Man of God was someone who—when I ask the question, '**Do you find your identity in Jesus Christ?**'—answers, 'Absolutely!'"

I saw a few heads nod, so I continued with my message. "What if I asked him, '**Do you love Jesus?**', and he answered, 'Absolutely!' And what if I asked, '**Do you want to spend the rest of your life learning to become just like Jesus?', and he said with confidence, 'Absolutely!'"

After sharing those three questions with the men at the retreat, I was prompted by the Lord to do something I had never thought of doing before I took the stage that weekend.

I had a small vial of olive oil in my pocket. I often carry a vial with me in case people ask me to pray for them while dealing with a trial or some sort of illness or health issue. That's when I would use a few drops of olive oil to anoint that person in keeping with the spirit of James 5:14 (NLT), which says, "Are any of you sick? You should call for the elders of the church to come and pray over you, anointing you with oil in the name of the Lord."

That morning, I said, "Men, I'm coming down to the front row, and I will look several of you right in the eye, point my finger right in your chest, anoint you with oil, and say, 'You are a Man of God!'

"Do not look away!" I continued. "**You now know what a Man of God is, and you are not confused about what constitutes a Man of God anymore.** So when I call you a Man of God, I want you to look right back at me in the eye and say firmly, 'Absolutely!'"

I went down to the first row and anointed five guys with oil, calling each one of them a Man of God. Each looked me in the eye and answered, "Absolutely!"

After anointing the five, I was out of time because lunch was being served. I told the other 175 men that I would get to them another time and returned to the stage to close in prayer and thank the Lord for the meal we were about to enjoy.

When I finished, I got my notes together and began to walk off the stage. I was startled by what I saw next. A half-dozen young guys had formed a single-file line. Someone said, "You had better get your oil back out!"

So I did, and I started anointing these men. And as I performed this simple act, God gave me a word of encouragement or affirmation for each one. Then more and more men started lining up. The line got longer and longer until it stretched all the way around the room.

There must have been a hundred men lined up. For the next hour, I patiently anointed each of the men and shared an encouraging word. They didn't mind delaying lunch, and I realized I was experiencing a true work of God that morning. **The Lord gave me an opportunity to minister to men in a unique way that touched their hearts.**

The next morning, a Sunday, I asked one of the young men why he had stood in line to be anointed with oil and hear that he was a Man of God. I was curious because men do not queue up in long lines voluntarily and do everything they can to avoid long waits. His quick response was to the point: **"I wanted to become a Man of God."**

A REMINDER ON THE WRIST

Two weeks after that retreat, there was a knock at the front door of my home. I opened it to find a young man standing there.

"Pastor McKenzie, a mutual friend gave me your address. I have something I want to give you." The young man then handed me a camouflage wristband with an inscription that read "Man of God."

"Pastor, you may not remember me, but you anointed me a Man of God at our men's retreat. I had these rubber wristbands made up so I can give one to all of the men who were anointed Men of God. We do not want to forget what God did there and who we are."

I was genuinely pleased and impressed. "What a brilliant idea. Where I can order some of those wristbands?" I asked.

When we present this teaching at men's conferences, we ask our men to answer three questions that I mentioned earlier before we put a Man of God wristband on them. These questions help men understand what they are agreeing to when they become a Man of God. Let's review them here:

1. Do you find your identity in Jesus Christ?

When we speak of a man's identity, we are talking about who you are. What are the traits, values, and beliefs that make you different or distinguishable from others? What is your defining character trait and personality like?

A man typically finds his identity in what he does for a living, how much he earns, or what he accomplishes. Maybe he is a tech wizard, a scratch golfer, a creative cook, or an accomplished musician. Or maybe he's proud to call himself a family man.

Houses, cars, and possessions don't last, however, if that's what you find your identity in. Youthful looks fade, if you think you're handsome and attractive to others. And if you find your identity in your family—which is a good thing—what will happen if and when you lose your parents, your wife, or one of your children before you leave this Earth?

When it comes to becoming a Man of God, you want to place your hopes and dreams in something that can *never* be taken away, which is Someone who has promised never to leave you or abandon you. Someone you can feel secure in.

Remember, Jesus is the Creator of all things. He created a system that works beautifully, if followed according to the directions He has given us in the Bible, His user's manual. That is security.

Jesus said that in this fallen, sinful world, we will have sorrows, sadness, and tribulations. That is the human condition.

What Jesus wants you to do is build your life on a Rock that can never be taken away from you. He instructs you to not just survive but to thrive in this world. God has given you all that you need to live on a new, higher level with Him. You can live a protected, successful life and be provided for in every way.

This is why we preach that a man's true security can only be found in Jesus Christ, especially His eternal security.

Jesus confirmed this in John 14:6 (NIV) when He said, "I am the way, the truth, and the life. No one comes to the Father except through Me."

Writing to the Philippians, Paul put it this way: "For me to live is Christ, to die is gain" (Philippians 1:21, NIV).

The secure Man of God has considered his priorities and what he should put first in his life. He has decided the most important thing he can do is to keep the Kingdom of God in its rightful place of preeminence and then let the chips fall where they may.

Jesus promised that if you do this, and all the other things in your life, including things that tend to be most anxious, then you will be provided for in His way and in His good timing.

This Man of God knows that he is saved. He is a citizen of the Kingdom of heaven. This world is not his final destination. He knows that Jesus will never change. He knows he is saved and nothing or no one can take that away from Him. There is no confusion about that. He knows that God has a tailor-made plan for his life, a life designed with his best interests in mind, and no one can change that. He has perfect clarity on that.

The Man of God hangs on Jesus' words in this Scripture:

"Do not store up for yourselves treasures on earth, where moths and rust eat them, and where thieves break in and steal. **But store up for yourselves treasures in heaven**, *where moths and rust do not destroy, and where thieves do not break in and steal. For where your treasure is, there your heart will be also."*

—Matthew 6:19-21 (NIV)
with boldface added for emphasis

The Message translation says it more plainly but just as effectively:

"It's obvious isn't it? The place where your treasure is, is the place where you will most want to be, and end up being."

Heed these words, my friend. Think about where you are storing treasure for the next life—not here on Earth. Cherish these words from Jesus:

"Anyone who listens to my teaching and follows it is wise, like a person who builds a house on solid rock. Though the rain comes in torrents and the floodwaters rise and the winds beat against that house, it won't collapse because it is built on bedrock. But anyone who hears my teaching and doesn't obey it is foolish, like a person who builds a house on sand. When the rains and floods come and the winds beat against that house, it will collapse with a mighty crash."

Matthew 7:24-27 (NLT)

What Jesus is explaining here is that there are two foundations you can build your house or life on. You can build it on the Rock, and He is the Rock. Or, you can build it on sand. Anything other than Him is sand and is from the devil.

The lesson is obvious. The choice is yours.

If you hear His words and believe He is the Messiah, the Lord of Lords and the King of Kings, and obey His word, you are building your life on Jesus, the Rock.

That's a foundation that will always stand, regardless of the storms, trials, wounds, horrific news, and everything this life can throw at you. He will see you through.

Let these verses encourage you:

"I am the Lord, and I do not change."

Malachi 3:6, NLT

Jesus Christ is the same yesterday, today, and forever.

Hebrews 13:8, NLT

"Do not be afraid, for I am with you. Don't be discouraged, for I am your God. I will strengthen you and help you. I will hold you up with my victorious right hand."

Isaiah 41:10, NLT

2. Do you love Jesus Christ?

I caution men before they answer, "Absolutely!", to think about what it truly means to love Jesus Christ.

One criticism of men's ministries is that most men are uncomfortable being asked if they can love their fellow man. The idea is that real men do not have to say "Hey, love ya, man" or even "I love you" to their wives.

The trouble is that the English language does not adequately express the word *love* when compared to the Greek language (the language the apostle Paul wrote in), which has four different words for love, each with a subtle but different meaning.

The first Greek word for love is *eros*, which is perhaps most commonly understood. *Eros*, as described by author Ed Wheat in his book, *Love Life*, is a passionate, romantic, and physical love that yearns to unite with and desires to possess the beloved. The truth is men in general have a hard time expressing any kind of love other than *eros* or sexual love. In fact, when men hear the word "love," most guys immediately think of sex. After all, "making love" is one of the most common terms used when speaking of sexual intercourse.

The next is *storge* (pronounced *stor-gay*), which is comprised of natural affection and a sense of belonging to each other. *Storge* love meets needs and meets feelings that we belong to something bigger than us and are part of a close-knit circle in which people care and give utmost loyalty to each other. *Storge* love is the love that a family feels for each other, or the love that teammates might share.

The next type of love is *phileo*, which is the love of relationship, friendship, or of a cherished friend. *Phileo* love says to a cherished friend, *I will trust you and confide in you things that I cannot or will not share with another person*, with the hope that his friend will trust him in the same way. Where *eros* makes lovers, *phileo* makes best friends—brotherly love. This is why Philadelphia is known as the "City of Brotherly Love."

The fourth word for love is *agape*, which involves faithfulness, commitment, and good will, and is the most common word used for *love* in the New Testament. The greatest example of *agape* love is Jesus Christ, who willingly went to the Cross to die for our sins.

Love Jesus with all your heart, with all your faithfulness, and with all your commitment. And as much as you can love Jesus, He loves you more!

3. Do you want to spend the rest of your life learning to become just like Jesus Christ?

This is the third and last question we ask men who want to become a Man of God. In other words, what price are you willing to pay to become just like Jesus?

There are a lot of Scripture verses that help to explain this question, but we love this one from the Amplified Bible the best:

> **Now may the God of peace Himself sanctify you through and through** [that is, separate you from profane and vulgar things, make you pure, and whole, and undamaged—consecrated to Him—set apart for His purpose]; and may your spirit and soul and body be kept complete and [be found] blameless at the coming of our Lord Jesus Christ.
>
> Faithful and absolutely trustworthy is He who is calling you [to Himself for your salvation], and He will do it [He will fulfill His call by making you holy, guarding you, watching over you, and protecting you as His own].
>
> 1 THESSALONIANS 5:23-24 (AMPLIFIED BIBLE)
with boldface added for emphasis

So, to sum up, if you find your identity in Christ, love Jesus, and want to spend the rest of your life getting to know Him better through reading the Bible, then step up and receive a dab of anointing oil.

We now pronounce you a Man of God!

DISCUSSION STARTER QUESTIONS:

❯ How do you feel about knowing that you don't have to work so hard to get God's approval?

❯ How do you feel about knowing that your sin doesn't alter God's love for you?

❯ What does God mean when He said in the Bible (in Deuteronomy, Joshua, and Hebrews), "I will never leave you or forsake you"?

PETE'S PRAYER

Father, as I seek to find my identity in You—to search the depths of what it means to truly love You and to spend the rest of my life learning to become just like You—I just have one thing to ask. Help! Because I really do want to be Your man and all that it means. Thank you, Father.

13
HEARING THE TRUTH
ABOUT JESUS

Since I (Pete) started investing myself in ministering to men, I've had the great privilege of using my small vial of oil to anoint more than 7,000 men as Men of God. This includes men from all over the state of California where I live, as well as in towns and cities across the United States and men's groups in Europe and Africa.

That number could be far more because early in the development of the Influencer's ministry, the Lord showed me an important detail. One time when I was meeting with a significant number of men from a church or community-wide group, He told me that it wouldn't be my responsibility to anoint the men from that group of believers. That responsibility would belong to the local pastors, elders, or men's ministry team in that church. When people take responsibility, they take ownership.

What God has shown me about myself and every other man who knows Christ is that **He understands who we are and loves us as His men**. A Man of God believes in His ability to take ordinary men and do extraordinary things through them by the power of the Holy Spirit, when we give Him something to work with, of course. **That often happens when we step out in faith.**

God understands our struggles to live what we profess to believe. **He is calling us, by His grace and mercy, to become Men of God for such a time as this.**

So, as we come to a close in *Cracking the Man Code*, I want you to ask yourself:

↗ What type of man are you?

↗ If someone really wanted to get to know you, what would he need to know?

Phil and I have already established that men tend to find their identities in their work, their family, their possessions, and many other things that are temporary. Those seem like a foundation for life, but they really aren't a solid foundation at all.

So, let me suggest how a true Man of God would answer the question about what type of man he is:

If you really want to know me, then you would need to know that Jesus Christ is the Lord of my life to the point that nothing in my life makes sense apart from Him. In light of this, I am not confused about who I am.

I am a Man of God. Absolutely! I have been put on this Earth to know Him and to make Him known. I am not ashamed of the gospel and have made the Bible the final authority in my life. I'm committed to ordering my life in obedience to what He teaches me. In other words, I do not judge the Bible by what is happening in the world around me. **I judge the world by the truth and insight I learn in the Bible.**

In light of His claim on my life, **I'm committed to linking my life together with other men who are chasing after Christ.** I see them as my best friends, my brothers, and my fellow travelers on this journey.

You need to know that **I am committed to becoming a man of prayer**, which is a demonstration of my humble and childlike total dependence on Him for everything.

In light of all of this and more, I am also not confused about where I'm going. **I place my faith in His promise of**

eternity because He died on the Cross for me to forgive my sins and secure my eternal salvation with Him in heaven.

SEEING YOURSELF

So, do you have a better idea of who you are? Are you comfortable in your skin?

In our ministry to men, we believe there are four categories of guys who hear the Gospel, or truth about Jesus. Where do you see yourself? The four categories are:

1. Those who reject the Gospel.

It's in vogue in this country to reject Jesus. Atheism is one form of that, but so are seeking out "other paths" to God—Eastern religions and mysticism, and a variety of self-guided ideas of "spirituality" like yoga and New Age. But too many men turn their backs on the gospel of Jesus Christ because they feel they don't need God. "I'm my own man," they say with hubris, revealing their pride, which is firmly rooted in the old Man Code.

2. Those who hear with the head but not with the heart.

What we mean by this second category of men is that they believe what the church says about getting saved, but they don't have an assurance of eternal life with Christ because they have a works-based view of salvation, meaning they have to "be good" or "do good things" to atone for the stupid stuff or bad things they do in their lives.

Sure, they understand that Jesus died for their sins, but it's all in their heads and not their hearts, meaning their lives haven't really changed and they haven't applied that knowledge to how they live.

3. Those who think they are saved but . . . .

The third category refers to those who Jesus talked about in Matthew 7:21 (NLT) when He said, "Not everyone who calls out to me, 'Lord! Lord!' will enter the Kingdom of heaven. **Only those who do the will of my Father in heaven will enter** . . . But I will reply, 'I never knew you. Get away from me, you who break God's laws.'"

What Jesus is saying is that your entrance into heaven won't be determined by what you say to Him. Instead, the only kind of person who enters the Kingdom of heaven will be those who *do* what He says—the person who does the will of God.

So what is the will of God? The ultimate will of God is that men would be saved, not by doing something but by being something. God's will is that we believe in Jesus, His Son, and He made that clear in Acts 4:12 (NLT), which says, "There is salvation in no one else! God has given no other name under heaven by which we must be saved."

God also spelled things out in the classic verse from John 3:16 (NIV), "For God so loved the world, that He gave His only begotten Son, that whoever believes in Him shall not perish, but have eternal life." And then in Ephesians 2:8-9 (NIV), the apostle Paul writes, "For by grace you have been saved, through faith—and this is not from yourselves, it is the gift of God; not by works, so that no one can boast."

4. Those who know they are saved, forgiven, and are going to spend eternity in heaven with their Savior.

The fourth and final category refers to men—we hope this includes you—who are Men of God.

These are the men described in 1 John 5:13-14 (NLT) in which the apostle John says, "I have written this to you who believe in the name of the Son of God, so that you may know you have eternal life. And we are confident that he hears us whenever we ask for anything that pleases him."

John is describing people who know about Jesus with conviction and confidence, which means there is security. They really know they are God's children because they believe God is their father.

The confident believer is never perfect, which is why this quest to know Him is never about perfection or any form of pursuit of perfection. This means that you know you are saved by the grace of God through faith in Jesus. The spirit of God bears witness in your heart. You are loved, forgiven, and assured by Jesus that He will be waiting to greet you in heaven with these words: "Well done, my good and faithful servant" (Matthew 25:23, NLT).

So, it is time to ask you this key question: **What category are you in? What category do you want to be in?**

Listen, we're all on a journey. I (Pete) will never forget the time when I was playing minor league baseball in North Carolina and I read *Impact Player: Leaving a Lasting Legacy On and Off the Field* by New York Yankee second baseman Bobby Richardson. Bobby played on the great Yankee teams of the 1950s and 1960s. After retiring from baseball, Bobby, being an outspoken Christian, played a vital role in the creation of the Fellowship of Christian Athletes (FCA) and Baseball Chapel, which still today ministers to MLB and minor league players.

I loved baseball at the time I read *Impact Player*. What I realized for the first time in my life was that I could be a professional baseball player *and* an uncompromising Christian at the same time.

I was also exhausted with my own sin, so I poured out this prayer, saying, "Lord, I'm a total failure at living this Christian stuff, and I know I can't keep the rules. I can't live this life. I'm tired. I know I'm not the man You created me to be, but I want to be. Will you make me that man?"

That's the night I came to Jesus. That's the night I received forgiveness. That's the night I got to know Jesus and know Him in a way I cannot explain.

I also received several priceless things from the Lord that night—forgiveness for my sins, eternal life with Him, and the knowledge that His grace was sufficient.

Phil, my writing colleague with *Cracking the Man Code*, told me that he wishes that he shared the same conviction earlier in his life. He shared this with me:

> I tried to manage sin and failed, probably still do. I was about twenty-two years old when I gave my life to God, but I only gave Him about 50 percent of the good stuff. I kept the rest of my sinful life even though God made it clear that it was not working.
>
> A decade later, I made a big change, and this time I gave 90 percent of myself. But I knowingly and unknowingly held tightly to long-standing sin and anger. It didn't take long for me to realize that wasn't working either.
>
> Then I did what Pete talks about in this book and which Scripture sums up so well. I invited God into *all* of my life—the good and the flawed. I asked Him to take away the old me. I became a new creation in Christ and backed it up with a commitment to a daily relationship with Jesus. I'm still on that daily journey, but what a difference! I'm surely an imperfect man, but I know I'm a loved child of God.

Maybe you know that you're *not* the man God created you to be. But you want to be a Man of God. You want God to make you into that man. You want to be saved.

If you want the assurance of eternal life with Him, there is a prayer for you. It's commonly called the Sinner's Prayer.

Maybe God is attracting you to this kind of prayer or commitment by using a problem or a trial or something that is personal to you.

With everything swirling around in life, **now is the time to settle**

down with Jesus and allow His peace and strength to reign in your life.

We invite you to say this simple prayer right now:

Lord, I'm a total failure at living this Christian stuff. I can't keep the rules. I can't live this life. I'm tired. I know I'm not the man you created me to be. But I want to be. Will you make me that man? A Man of God?

If you prayed this prayer and are ready to move forward, it's important to seek support. **Please contact us at our website, www.InfluencersWest.org,** and Bill Kauble or another leader will follow up with you.

Getting connected with a local Bible-based church is the most important first step you can take—especially one that ministers to men. God made us to be in community with each other. Do not take that lightly or underestimate the importance of relationships with other believers. Commit yourself to finding a local Bible-based church and men's ministry near you today.

A FINAL THOUGHT

We close with a prayer that is close to the hearts of the guys who started and lead Influencer's West Men's Ministry:

A Prayer for Men of God

Lord, give us men.

Men with stout hearts and fire in their eyes.

Men who fear nothing but You,
and who owe nothing to anyone but acts of love.

Lord, give us men, men who are willing to live and die for You, who name the name of Christ and live for His glory.

Lord, give us men who know Your voice and whose greatest delight is to obey. We ask that You give us men who are slow to anger, quick to listen, and eager to forgive.

Lord, give us men who love their wives and honor You in their homes, men who are living apostles of salt and light to all they know and meet, men whose sacrifice, service, and love are renown and are known to have spent time with You.

Lord, give us this kind of men, for the world is desperate for them.

Lord, give us men of faith and action, who have eternity in their hearts and only You as their focus, passion, and reason for living, men of whom the world is not worthy.

Lord, we know these men are rare and few, but they know that You use ordinary men to do extraordinary things through Your power. We know that You use foolish men to shame the wise and weak men who because of You become strong. We know that you use men who are known more for their availability than their ability, men who choose to decrease so that You may increase.

Lord, this seems like an impossible request, but these are the kind of men You make when they give their lives in total abandonment and absolute trust to You.

Lord, give us men, thousands of men who give their lives in that same abandonment and absolute trust.

And finally, Lord, let me be a man like this and among men like this.

Lord, let me be that man.

DISCUSSION STARTER QUESTIONS

❯ What thoughts popped into your mind when you read that Jesus understands all about you and still loves you?

❯ What's the truth and insight in the Bible that leads to becoming a Man of God?

❯ On a scale of 1-10, with 10 being totally confident, how confident are you that Jesus is Lord of your life?

❯ Have you given your life to Jesus? Would you like to read the Sinner's Prayer again and invite him into your life right now?

If you said it and meant it, contact us at www.InfluencersWest.org right now. We will share your joy and would love to follow up with you.

PETE'S FINAL PRAYER

Lord, every act of spiritual thought, word, and activity
is orchestrated by You, for apart from You, I know I can do
nothing. It's You who gives me the grace and faith to believe.
Lord, in my heart of hearts I desire to be a Man of God.
I ask this in faith and forsake all fear because You never
honor fear, but You always honor faith in You.

THE MAN OF GOD MANIFESTO

I am a Man of God!

I no longer have to "do" something to own that title. I no longer trust in my own human ability to be the man God created me to be. I own the title by trusting in God's grace and by allowing Christ to live His life in me.

I am a Man of God!

I have finally made peace with reality that I cannot defeat my sin by my sincere efforts. I am accountable to Jesus, and He is stronger than my sin. As I abandon myself to Him by faith, He will defeat the sin in me that I cannot control myself.

I am a Man of God!

I am not confused about who I am, who I belong to, why I'm here, where I'm going, or how I'm going to get there. That has all been settled in my personal relationship with Jesus Christ.

I am a Man of God!

I no longer believe that I am who the world says I am because I know I am who God says I am, and I'm believing and accepting this truth that has changed my life forever.

I am a Man of God!

I no longer have to search for significance or importance because my meaning and value in life is found in Jesus Christ. He gives my life great meaning and immeasurable worth.

I am a Man of God!

I no longer need to find my peace in the approval of others, for though I am far from perfect, I have found grace in Jesus' unconditional love, acceptance, and approval of me.

I am a Man of God!

I no longer have to seek for influence or power because Jesus gives me influence as He empowers me to make sacrifices for others.

I am a Man of God!

I know the meaning of a life lived successfully because Jesus is my model, and He accomplished all that His Father had for Him to do.

I am a Man of God!

I know that I only have one life to live and that it will soon be passed. In light of that, the great eternal truth is that only what I do in Jesus Christ, for Jesus Christ, and through Jesus Christ will last.

I am a Man of God! Absolutely!

*"But you, man of God . . . pursue righteousness, godliness, faith, love, endurance and gentleness. **Fight the good fight of the faith.** Take hold of the eternal life to which you were called . . ."*

—1 TIMOTHY 6: 11-12, NIV
with boldface added for emphasis

A Man of God Will Not Forget

I am a Man of God

I have been bought with a price

I am not my own

I know who I am

I know who I belong to

I know who I serve

I know why I'm here

I know where I'm going

I know who will get me there

I will serve in Jesus' strength

I will serve to honor Him

I will not forget that I am a man of God

And that I live for Christ and the Gospel

I am a Man of God

ABSOLUTELY!

PETE MCKENZIE
Originally written July 25, 2007

ACKNOWLEDGEMENTS

A s we mentioned at the start of *Cracking the Man Code*, this book has been a labor of love for more than five years. Without the encouragement of countless men in our lives, along with the support of our wives, *Cracking the Man Code* wouldn't see the light of day.

We suppose the first person to thank is Jim Litchfield, an Influencers West group leader from La Habra Heights, California. Jim introduced us to each other ten years ago at an Influencers West meeting in Orange County in Southern California. That first meeting inspired Phil to start an Influencers West chapter in La Crescenta, California.

The Influencers West leadership team of Bill Kauble, Thad Montgomery, and Gary Schrey have been servant leaders who have inspired us over the years. A pastor and good friend, Andy Wilson, who helped launch that group in La Crescenta, reminds us of the impact of guys gathering together to read the Bible and pray.

Great men like Jim Larsen, Jim Granier, Jerry White, Mark Williams, John Holmquist, Ron Rickets, Geoff Bryan, Doug Given, Don Empey, and Evan O'Meara gave us tons of encouragement. They read early versions of this book at the La Crescenta Influencers West weekly meetings.

Finally, we are grateful for veteran writer Mike Yorkey, who collaborated with us on *Cracking the Man Code*. He is a truly gifted writer and a close friend who did a fabulous job with this manuscript. Heidi Moss also did a wonderful job proofing the manuscript.

ABOUT THE AUTHORS

PETE MCKENZIE oversees and encourages ministries to men in the western half of the United States for The Influencers. Since 2006, he has counseled, mentored, and acted as a life coach for men chasing after Jesus Christ, with the view of raising up Men of God for such a time as this.

Pete grew up in Birmingham, Alabama, and won a baseball scholarship to Auburn University. Following graduation, he played several years of professional baseball in the minor leagues. He then moved into ministry as the principal of a Christian school and then became a pastor, eventually moving to Europe in the 1980s and overseeing a ministry that traveled to five countries behind the Iron Curtain. As director, Pete trained pastors and key laymen in discipleship methods and church-planting strategies in the last years before the Berlin Wall came down in 1989.

Pete married his high school sweetheart, Suzan, and they raised three children, Jenny, Chris, and Patrick. They were ministry partners, and Suzan was a real trooper, whether they were living in Alabama, Germany, or Southern California. Tragically, Suzan died in the summer of 2017, a few weeks short of their fiftieth wedding anniversary. They have six grandchildren.

PHIL VAN HORN is a baseball and entertainment agent at Integrity Sports & Artists Agency in Pasadena, California.

He's a former college baseball coach at Cal State Northridge and the University of Southern California. Major league baseball's 2017 MVP Giancarlo Stanton credits Phil's hitting training with a significant role in his breakthrough as a prospect during his high school years. (Stanton grew up near Phil.)

Phil began a career in media as a sportswriter while in high school in his hometown of Indianapolis, Indiana. After attending nearby Ball State University, Phil was hired by CNN and spent fifteen years living in Atlanta, where he also worked on the air for Turner Sports and ESPN. Phil met his wife, Lecia, while working at CNN. Their children, Kari and Brandon, were born in Atlanta.

After moving to Lecia's hometown of Los Angeles, Phil won an Emmy for a local L.A. show on the 2000 Sydney Olympics.

Today, he and his family live in Altadena, California, where Lecia is a TV news journalist in Los Angeles.

MIKE YORKEY is the author or co-author of more than one hundred books with more than 2 million copies in print. He has collaborated with Cyndy Feasel, an ex-NFL wife, in *After the Cheering Stops*; the Chicago Cubs' Ben Zobrist and his wife, Julianna, a Christian music artist, in *Double Play*; KKLA talk-show show host Frank Sontag in *Light the Way Home*; Washington Redskins quarterback Colt McCoy and his father, Brad, in *Growing Up Colt*; San Francisco Giants pitcher Dave Dravecky in *Called Up*; San Diego Chargers placekicker Rolf Benirschke in *Alive & Kicking*; tennis star Michael Chang in *Holding Serve*; and paralyzed Rutgers' defensive tackle Eric LeGrand in *Believe: My Faith and the Tackle That Changed My Life;* and pop singers Marilyn McCoo and Billy Davis Jr. in *Up, Up, and Away*. Mike is also the co-author of the internationally bestselling *Every Man's Battle* series with Steve Arterburn and Fred Stoeker. He has written several fiction books, including *The Swiss Courier* and *Chasing Mona Lisa*.

He and his wife, Nicole, are the parents of two adult children and make their home in Encinitas, California.

Mike's website is www.mikeyorkey.com.

INVITE PETE MCKENZIE TO SPEAK TODAY

Pete McKenzie is a dynamic, thoughtful speaker with a passion to talk to men about life's most important issues—their relationship with Christ, their marriages, and the importance of being in a men's group. Pete, who has traveled around the world speaking before tens of thousands of men, is available to speak at various men's gatherings as well as weekend retreats.

If you, your men's group, men's ministry, or church would be interested in having Pete speak at your event, please contact Phil Van Horn at ballphild@gmail.com or by texting 818-517-5880.